THE
TITANIC
AWARDS®

THE
TITANIC
AWARDS®

★ ★ ★

Celebrating the
Worst of Travel

Doug Lansky

A PERIGEE BOOK

A PERIGEE BOOK
Published by the Penguin Group
Penguin Group (USA) Inc.
375 Hudson Street, New York, New York 10014, USA
Penguin Group (Canada), 90 Eglinton Avenue East, Suite 700, Toronto, Ontario M4P 2Y3, Canada
(a division of Pearson Penguin Canada Inc.)
Penguin Books Ltd., 80 Strand, London WC2R 0RL, England
Penguin Group Ireland, 25 St. Stephen's Green, Dublin 2, Ireland (a division of Penguin Books Ltd.)
Penguin Group (Australia), 250 Camberwell Road, Camberwell, Victoria 3124, Australia
(a division of Pearson Australia Group Pty. Ltd.)
Penguin Books India Pvt. Ltd., 11 Community Centre, Panchsheel Park, New Delhi—110 017, India
Penguin Group (NZ), 67 Apollo Drive, Rosedale, North Shore 0632, New Zealand
(a division of Pearson New Zealand Ltd.)
Penguin Books (South Africa) (Pty.) Ltd., 24 Sturdee Avenue, Rosebank, Johannesburg 2196, South Africa

Penguin Books Ltd., Registered Offices: 80 Strand, London WC2R 0RL, England

While the author has made every effort to provide accurate telephone numbers and Internet addresses at
the time of publication, neither the publisher nor the author assumes any responsibility for errors, or for
changes that occur after publication. Further, the publisher does not have any control over and does not
assume any responsibility for author or third-party websites or their content.

First edition: May 2010

Library of Congress Cataloging-in-Publication Data

Lansky, Doug.
    The Titanic awards : celebrating the worst of travel / Doug Lansky.— 1st ed.
        p.   cm.
    ISBN 978-0-399-53584-0
    1. Travel—Humor.   2. Travel—Anecdotes.   I. Title.
    PN6231.T7L27   2010
    910.402'07—dc22   2009053891

PRINTED IN THE UNITED STATES OF AMERICA

10   9   8   7   6   5   4   3   2   1

Most Perigee books are available at special quantity discounts for bulk purchases for sales promotions,
premiums, fund-raising, or educational use. Special books, or book excerpts, can also be created to fit
specific needs. For details, write: Special Markets, Penguin Group (USA) Inc., 375 Hudson Street, New York,
New York 10014.

*To all the travelers who overcame annoyances
and obstacles to make it to their destinations and then
willingly decided to set out traveling again*

When things go wrong, travel gets more interesting. If everything goes exactly as planned, the trip may be all right, but is it the trip you'll tell people about for years to come? Probably not. Travelers who can stay flexible and roll with the glitches do well, even thrive, when adversity strikes.

—Jim Benning, cofounder and editor of WorldHum.com

CONTENTS

NOTE TO READERS

To be honest, *The Titanic Awards* has less of a story line than most Ikea instruction manuals and, as such, was never intended to be read in one fell swoop, cover to cover. As with a jar of coffee that's best consumed a cup at a time over many days or weeks, you probably don't want three overstimulating gallons of dubious travel tales at one sitting. This book is, perhaps, best kept by the bed, by the toilet, or somewhere it can easily be read in reasonable doses.

INTRODUCTION

If you've ever wedged yourself into an airplane seat, checked your luggage, or reserved a room in a hotel, you know there are few perfect trips on this planet. Something invariably goes wrong. At times, very wrong. It may only be a computer scheduling glitch you can almost understand or an overzealous airport security officer patting down frail senior citizens. But other times there's outright incompetence at almost incomprehensible levels. Such as when Iranian refugee Mehran Karimi Nasseri was famously kept in limbo in the Charles de Gaulle International Airport for 18 years. Or, in a less drastic display of ineptitude, when a Taliban-esque Southwest Airlines attendant denied a female passenger from taking a flight because he found her miniskirt/tank top/cardigan sweater combo to be "too revealing" to fly* (page 50). The behind-the-scenes practices can be just as baffling, such as when Nepal Airlines attempted to solve some technical issues with a Boeing 757 engine by sacrificing two goats to appease the sky god Akash Bhairab** (page 12), or when Northwest Airlines baggage handlers were caught on security camera tossing about items coming off an airplane in a manner more befitting the Harlem Globetrotters, including high blind lobs while facing backward. (See the video clip at TitanicAwards.com.)

The Titanic Awards seeks to take a different approach to these often spectacular underachievements in the travel industry . . . by celebrating them.

Unlike with *The Darwin Awards*, no one needs to die to qualify for

---

* MSNBC, September 11, 2007

** Reuters, BBC, September 5, 2007

entry into this book. However, many of the Titanic nominees do share a common flair for stupidity, an impressive knack for absentmindedness, and an entertaining neglect for safety.

Over the last decades, the travel industry and media have unwittingly teamed up to create the gap this book aspires to fill. I read a lot of travel sections, travel sites, and travel magazines, and I realized one day I was getting punch-drunk on how fantastic everything was. There's just so much "Escape," "Undiscovered," "Quaint," "Top 10 Most Amazing . . . ," "Secret Beaches," "Incredible Islands," "Savvy," "Frugal," "Best Ever." These adjectives just don't connect with most of my experiences on the road—life, misadventure, and a dose of Murphy's Law often get in the way.

You see critical reviews of books, movies, and plays in the media, but when was the last time you saw someone say a destination was awful? Or that they disliked a fancy new resort? Or that a pair of new travel sandals was worthless? I don't expect the cover of *Islands* magazine to boast "Top 5 Islands That Totally Suck!" or the *New York Times* to lead the travel section with "36 Hours Bored Out of My F*cking Mind in Iowa."

(Though that would probably be a fun read.)

But there must be a few destinations, resorts, or attractions that deserve a more disparaging eye.

There's a good reason we don't see them. For starters, travel, according to the United Nations World Tourism Organization, is the world's largest industry, transporting 903 million people internationally last year (5 to 10 million moving about internationally at any given moment on our planet). The aviation industry alone transports 2.2 billion passengers each year (domestically and internationally, using 23,000 aircraft and 3,754 airports), generates 32 million jobs, and accounts for 8 percent of world gross domestic product.

In other words, there are large financial interests involved. And these are many of the same financial interests that are bankrolling the travel sections and travel magazines. The ads don't necessarily dictate what the travel publications can say, but they definitely influence what they can't (or won't). In other words, might they conveniently decide not to cover a story detrimental to one of their advertisers? Sure. Although it won't likely feel that obvious, even to the editors; they're simply deciding, they would say, to cover another story they find more compelling, more positive. Many editors (and their ad sales teams) believe that travel writing is where people go to escape. They're largely in the business of fulfilling dreams, especially all those dreamy photos of desolate villages on the edge of the Sahara, hot air balloon rides above wildebeest migrations on the Serengeti, and treks that offer mouth-dropping views of Mount Everest. Their readers don't want to hear about anything negative or overly critical. The *San Francisco Chronicle*'s former travel editor John Flinn has a nice phrase for it. "As a means of stoking an almost feverish level of wanderlust, these voluptuously alluring publications are every bit as effective as *Playboy* and *Penthouse* are at instigating lust of a different sort. They're adventure-travel porn. And I mean that in only the best way."

In terms of the destinations, editors may state—and rightly so—that you can't pan an entire genre. Condemning a destination is akin to saying all children's books are poorly written. "And if we have to narrow it down to individual restaurants and hotels and tour guides," says *Charlotte Observer* travel editor John Bordsen, "why should we choose a bad one to critique instead of helping readers by telling them about the good ones?"

It's not just the editors who avoid harsh reviews. Many travel writers are plugged in to the travel industry's matrix as well. Some believe that making the reader want to go there is a sign of literary success, or they have taken free trips (or free VIP upgrades) and are afraid of getting blacklisted for future freebies by PR firms if their review is less than glowing. Often, it's a combination. Sometimes travel writers who try to convey less flattering information find that their editors aren't interested, or that to cleverly craft the report so it doesn't come across as whiny, they have to use so many words that the piece no longer fits into the allotted space.

And when it does, other problems can arise. Martin Dunford, former publisher of the Rough Guides series, put it this way: "Our Provence author wrote bitterly about the number of 'dollar-dripping dickheads' that she came across on the Côte d'Azur. Not sure who else she expected to come across in Cannes but in the old days we used to cherish such lines; nowadays people get offended by stuff like that."

The problem, of course, is that if you eliminate all critical reviews for one reason or another, travel is getting an exemption from journalism, and we're left with publications serving as glorified travel brochures. That presents at least two issues: (1) it makes us feel all the more disappointed when our own trips are less than perfect; and (2) the media is not holding poorly run airlines, hotels, restaurants, tour operators, tourist boards, and their like accountable.

This book doesn't aspire to fill the accountability gap, but a few playful shots across the bow of the travel industry wouldn't hurt. Mostly, it hopes to show how a more celebratory format can allow us all to more readily embrace this often neglected (and highly entertaining) underbelly of travel. Besides sharing a few travel nightmares and learning we have a common lack of appreciation for certain sectors of the industry, *The Titanic Awards* should make it easier to cope the next time something goes wrong on your trip. And who knows, by casting a bit more light on the airlines (and others) who inflict the most suffering, the book may just provide a little more incentive for them to do something about it.

As for my own worst travels, I don't think I've ever had an entirely bad trip. I traveled full-time for nine years in about 120 countries, and I found that the worst things happened in small segments along the way. Here are just a few.

WORST J-WALKING: it wasn't just that I got run over by a car at a pedestrian crossing in Bangkok. I then had to hitchhike to a local hospital with a broken ankle and get myself back to my "base camp" in Europe for surgery. Perhaps the worst aspect was the combination of a painful, newly operated-on leg and amoebic dysentery (constantly having to go, rarely able to get there in time).

WORST WAKE-UP: 3:30 a.m., sleeping in a hammock deep in the Colombian rain forest. I was woken by some so-called head hunters in loincloths who actually started cutting my head with a machete while yelling at me. Turns out they were drunk on fermented corn juice and were just playing around. At least, that's how I reasoned it when I was still alive at breakfast.

WORST CONTINUOUS OVERLAND STRETCH: a nonstop, 52-hour haul from Goa to Calcutta by bus and train. They wouldn't sell me a ticket for part of the train journey, so I spent about five painfully sleep-deprived hours fleeing from the conductor.

WORST TOILET EXPERIENCE IN EUROPE: embarrassingly locking myself into a public toilet stall in a Dutch library and having to yell for help. I had left the handle in the door on the outside of the stall; I had no idea I needed to bring the handle with me to get out. I was eventually rescued by a passing urinator.

WORST TRANSPORT DELAY: waiting on an Amazon cargo ship parked in Manaus, Brazil, for four very hot and boring days while the captain was deciding when to leave. The harbor area was rife with sketchy characters, and people did get robbed, and we were all sleeping in hammocks strung up elbow to elbow, so nighttime felt like that scene from *Papillon* on the boat ride to the island prison. No one slept much.

WORST ALTITUDE SICKNESS: collapsing facedown 100 meters (328 feet) from the summit of Mount Cotopaxi in Ecuador and getting partially dragged down by the guide.

How Do You Win a Titanic Award?

There are three ways to win.

TITANIC SURVEY (READERS' CHOICE)

Winners are chosen by the voting public who complete the official Titanic Award Survey. The survey was taken by more than 2,000 people from more than 80 different countries over three months (though not everyone chose to answer every single question). They were directed to the survey from places like LonelyPlanet.com, *National Geographic Trav-*

eler's website, CNN.com, and various major newspaper travel sections around the world, including the *New York Times*, *USA Today*, and the *Sydney Morning Herald*. The opinions of these international travelers have been used to determine the nation with the most annoying tourists, rudest waiters, most confusing roads, cheapest tourists, and other subjective Titanic Winners.

Okay, now the disclaimer: As with most surveys, there's no way to know if the people taking ours were answering honestly, had forgotten to take their medication, or were just randomly clicking buttons. And even if we assume people made their best educated effort, there's no way everyone has been everywhere. And if voters are using personal experience (as they should), that means the most popular airlines, destinations, and so on are far more likely to make the list. However, if that were the only thing influencing the way people voted, the most known/visited places would win every time. But they didn't, so there seems to be a measure of reasoning behind the answers. Either way, please take the survey results with a grain of salt.

One more little disclaimer (as long as I've started): Although this book contains real news items and opinions, it is meant to be entertaining. When it states that some airline or city name is the "worst" or "most overrated" or "least appealing" or some such, this is a combination of opinion, a lighthearted approach, and a loosely used label.

Also, in some news items mentioned in the book, people were arrested, injured, or killed. These stories were covered by the news media because of their unusual nature and ties to travel/transportation—the same reason I found them compelling. This book does not wish to make light of the personal predicament or tragedy of those involved. For that reason, the last names of these travelers have been withheld. Yes, they're available to the general public in the various news sources. It just seemed that these unfortunate individuals may have already received more publicity than they ever wanted, and removing their last names helps this book highlight the story, not the person. The last names of various witnesses and spokespeople for airlines and hotels were, however, included, as they were either integral to the story or involved in a professional capacity.

Not too late for one more? Good. I wanted to mention the awards based on industry research that was not performed by Titanic Awards. For starters, we're going to assume that these professional statisticians and researchers did their data-gathering properly, which you have every right to feel is a rather large assumption. (It's somehow easier to believe that the airlines screwed up than that the people gathering the information about the airline screwups might have screwed up themselves.) Second, presenting their pregathered information was not as straightforward as you might think. When do you start measuring? Last quarter, last year, three years ago? This decision would likely produce three different Titanic Winners. Eventually, a decision was made to use the last full year ending at the most recent quarter for which there were data at the time of writing. Since not all quarters were equal (in terms of passenger traffic, for example), I ranked them for each quarter, then took the average ranking of the four quarters. So, yes, I was finally able to put my third-grade math skills to use.

OFFICIAL STUDY

Some winners are the result of an official study by an industry watch group or association. For example, the Federal Aviation Administration keeps official tabs on how much luggage each U.S. airline manages to lose.

EDITOR'S CHOICE

These winners are chosen by the editor for a specific travel incident. After scouring hundreds of news sources and thousands of web pages for obscure, offbeat, and sometimes tragic travel news stories, these winners were selected using some basic criteria: there should be a clear and present lack of sound judgment, noteworthy neglect, or admirable stupidity, and these travel tales must be documented by news sources, photographed, or videotaped. (The video category can be found exclusively online at TitanicAwards.com.)

ADDITIONAL NOMINATIONS

I've interviewed more than 75 travel writers, travel TV hosts, and leading travel bloggers for this book. If things go awry on most trips, I wondered what sort of travel nightmares professional travelers have accumulated over the years, often in remote parts of the world. Their roughly twitter-length "worst of" tales have been included throughout the book. Not only are their personal accounts and rants compelling (and were often cathartic for them to finally share) but they also show the diversity of opinion and the variety of locations where misadventures can be found.

As you sit back and enjoy their professional pitfalls and the under-achievements of the travel industry in the following pages, you may recall some of your own nightmare travel tales. If so, please share them at TitanicAwards.com. Tales can be added right to the comments of your favorite travel writer or a news piece that jogs your memory. Photos and video can be submitted by email.

PART 1

AIR TRAVEL

Motto of the U.S. airline industry: "We're Hoping to Have a
Motto Announcement in About an Hour."

—DAVE BARRY

When the first commercial jet, the de Havilland Comet, was introduced in 1952, it ushered in an entirely new concept that the
Wright Brothers never anticipated: air travel complaints. The modern
traveler could now brag of turbulence, delays, in-flight meals, and mis-
handled luggage. Both air travel and these surrounding issues gained
traction with the introduction of the Boeing 707s. Boeing created 1,010
"seven-oh-sevens," which dominated passenger air transport in the
1960s. In 1970, the Boeing 747 became the king of the skies, and it wasn't
dethroned until the Airbus A380 in 2005. You might look at it as basic
math: more and bigger planes means more passengers and more flights
and more delays and more lost luggage and more waiting.

Air travel may offer one of the safest modes of transport, but the
issues around it have not abated. Between cost cutting, the creation of
no-frills carriers, old planes finding new life in developing nations, com-
plicated baggage delivery systems, and overburdened airports, we've
entered the golden age of air travel complaints. And for good reason: for
all too many flights, former mainstays—such as comfort, timeliness,
and general good customer service—have gone the way of the DC-9 (out
of production after 41 years and nearly 2,500 planes built).

DUMBEST REASON TO GET THROWN OFF A PLANE

EDITOR'S CHOICE

WINNER

After an 11-hour layover at Bush Intercontinental Airport in Houston, Kate and her 19-month-old son, Garren, finally got on their Continental ExpressJet flight home. Kate was trying to keep her son occupied during the preflight procedures and pointed out another aircraft out the window. "Bye, bye, plane," Garren said. He repeated this many times while a flight attendant went over safety instructions.

After the safety demo, the flight attendant leaned over the man sitting in the aisle seat and said to the mom: "Okay, it's not funny anymore. You need to shut your baby up." Kate explained she was simply distracting her son until he fell asleep, which he would be doing shortly. The flight attendant suggested giving the child an allergy medication to help him sleep. Kate refused to drug her child at the flight attendant's request, and their discussion escalated into an argument.

The flight attendant told the captain that a woman had threatened her (Kate denied making any threats), so he agreed to taxi back to the airport. A witness on the flight said she heard the flight attendant brag to Kate that "We're going back to the gate." Other passengers came to the defense of Kate (and her now sleeping son) to try to keep them from getting thrown off, but to no avail. She was told the police would remove her if she didn't disembark immediately. Kate and her son had no choice but to exit the plane and try to find a place to spend the night.

An ExpressJet spokeswoman merely recited the standard line that any passenger compromising the safety of the other passengers or crew or undermining a crew member's authority may be removed from the aircraft. Though the airline was happy to explain to the media that they "take any complaints about these issues seriously." Source: ABC News

A man and his porn do not part ways easily. A Nationwide flight attendant should have considered this when she asked a male passenger known as A.C. to put away his adult magazine. The passenger and his porn were about to fly from Johannesburg to Cape Town when he was asked to desist from perusing the material. According to the airline's spokesperson Roger Whittle, the passenger "became abusive and threatened the cabin crew, using inappropriate language." (He told the flight attendant she was being f*cking rude.) This is why, Whittle explained, A.C. and his porn were kicked off the flight prior to departure. A.C. reportedly made an appointment to meet with his lawyer later that afternoon to decide on an appropriate course of action.

Source: *Independent Online* (South Africa), April 5, 2005

PERSONAL WORST

WORST AIRLINE *The service on most American Airlines flights makes Ryanair look like Concorde.*

—Martin Dunford, former publisher of the Rough Guides series

TITANIC AWARD

AIRPORT WITH MOST CONFUSING LAYOUT (OF 50 BIGGEST)

WINNER

London Heathrow

AFRICA/MIDDLE EAST WINNER: Dubai

ASIA WINNER: Bangkok

EUROPE WINNER: Heathrow

LATIN AMERICA WINNER: Mexico City

NORTH AMERICA WINNER: LAX (Los Angeles)

PACIFIC WINNER: Sydney

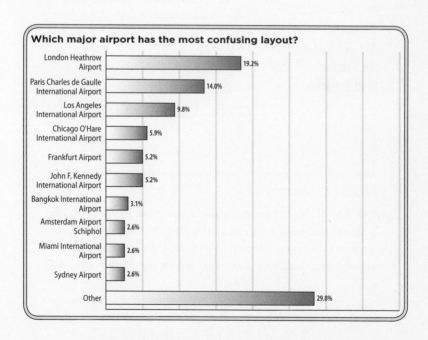

Which major airport has the most confusing layout?

Airport	%
London Heathrow Airport	19.2%
Paris Charles de Gaulle International Airport	14.0%
Los Angeles International Airport	9.8%
Chicago O'Hare International Airport	5.9%
Frankfurt Airport	5.2%
John F. Kennedy International Airport	5.2%
Bangkok International Airport	3.1%
Amsterdam Airport Schiphol	2.6%
Miami International Airport	2.6%
Sydney Airport	2.6%
Other	29.8%

TITANIC AWARD

EUROPEAN AIRLINE WITH MOST CONSISTENT DELAYS (SHORT- AND MEDIUM-HAUL FLIGHTS)

WINNER
Croatia Airlines

Its most impressive quarter was Q3 2007, when a noteworthy 57.5 percent of its flights had delays.

HONORABLE MENTIONS

- Scandinavia Airlines
- Alitalia, Luxair
- Air France
- British Airways

Source: *Association of European Airlines Consumer Report* (Most recent year with statistics available: Q2 2007–Q1 2008; calculation was based on average quarterly ranking)

PERSONAL WORST

WORST FLIGHT *Flew to Ireland despite a severe head cold. As the landing approached, I desperately yawned, huffed, etc. But as my wife gazed out the window at that gorgeous green countryside for the first time, my eardrum burst. Significant pain. (But there's good news—they grow back.)*

—Christopher Reynolds, travel writer for the *Los Angeles Times*

OFFICIAL STUDY

TITANIC AWARD

EUROPEAN AIRLINE WITH MOST CONSISTENTLY DELAYED LUGGAGE

WINNER

British Airways

Its most impressive quarter was Q3 2007, when it managed to delay 30 pieces of luggage per 1,000 transported.

HONORABLE MENTIONS

- TAP Portugal
- KLM
- Air France
- Alitalia

Source: *Association of European Airlines Consumer Report* (Most recent year with statistics available: Q2 2007–Q1 2008; calculation was made based on average quarterly ranking)

PERSONAL WORST

WORST FIRST-WORLD AIRPORT *This is an easy one. Miami. To me, it's the last flight out of Saigon every time I go through the place. The only redeeming thing in the entire airport is the great Cuban food at La Carreta, which you'll be eating since you stand an excellent chance of not going anywhere fast.*

—Peter Greenberg, investigative travel reporter and producer, served as correspondent for ABC's *Good Morning America* and travel editor for NBC's *Today* show

TITANIC AWARD

LEAST BOTHERSOME FLAMING 747 ENGINE

WINNER

British Airways (Flight 268)

When British Airways flight 268 departed Los Angeles en route to London with 352 passengers and 18 crew, the 747 pilot soon realized that only three of the four engines were operating. How did he know? Perhaps it was when the entire number two engine burst into flames before the plane even left L.A. County airspace. Faced with the choice of flying with three engines for the remaining 11 hours or dumping $30,000 in fuel to make an emergency landing (and possibly paying upwards of $275,000 to compensate passengers for a late arrival), the British Airways home office suggested the pilot go for it. The pilot then told the control tower in L.A. that he and his crew would try to "get as far as we can." The control tower officer, which had witnessed the flames coming from the plane, was stunned. Impressively, the plane nearly made it to London. Low fuel levels deterred that plan and forced the pilot to make a safe emergency landing in Manchester. Surprised by the decision? The Air Accident Investigation Branch, part of the UK's Department of Transport, found that continuing after an engine failure occurred on 15 other BA flights in the last five years. Source: *Guardian*, September 25, 2006

EDITOR'S
CHOICE

LEAST EXPERIENCED PILOT

WINNER

Anadolujet

A pilot flying a Boeing 737 for the Turkish airline Anadolujet left the cockpit to use the bathroom. No problem there. But he left the controls in the hands of a 15-year-old boy. Small problem.

The pilot was likely unaware of a similar incident in 1994 that killed 70 people on an Aeroflot flight when the pilot's son turned off the autopilot.

Anadolujet, much to its credit, sacked the pilot, but not before picking up a Titanic Award.

Source: *Mirror*, September 24, 2008

PERSONAL WORST

WORST AIRPORT   *The worst has to be in Douala, Cameroon. Aside from the bribes, there's the complete lack of air-conditioning, chairs, facilities, and organization. Charles de Gaulle runs a tough second.*

—Jane Wooldridge, travel editor of the *Miami Herald*

TITANIC AWARD

AIRPORT WITH WORST SECURITY (OF 50 BIGGEST)

WINNER

LAX (Los Angeles)

AFRICA/MIDDLE EAST WINNER: Dubai

ASIA WINNER: Kuala Lumpur

EUROPE WINNER: London Heathrow

LATIN AMERICA WINNER: Mexico City

NORTH AMERICA WINNER: LAX (Los Angeles)

PACIFIC WINNER: Sydney

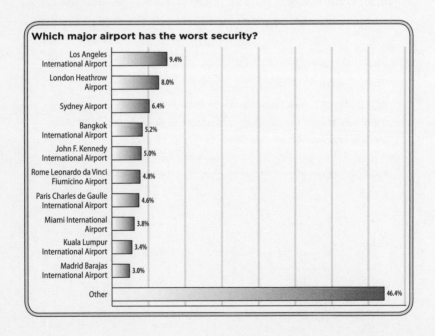

Which major airport has the worst security?

Airport	%
Los Angeles International Airport	9.4%
London Heathrow Airport	8.0%
Sydney Airport	6.4%
Bangkok International Airport	5.2%
John F. Kennedy International Airport	5.0%
Rome Leonardo da Vinci Fiumicino Airport	4.8%
Paris Charles de Gaulle International Airport	4.6%
Miami International Airport	3.8%
Kuala Lumpur International Airport	3.4%
Madrid Barajas International Airport	3.0%
Other	46.4%

LEAST LIFE-THREATENING EMERGENCY LANDING

EDITOR'S CHOICE

WINNER

US Airways

On a cross-country flight, a 50-year-old male passenger decided to disrobe while sitting in his seat in the back of the aircraft.

The US Airways pilot faced the prospect of flying with a naked man in the back of the plane or diverting the flight to Albuquerque and making an unscheduled landing to have the man covered as soon as possible (apparently, the plane's blankets wouldn't suffice, nor would putting his tray table down).

In America, nudity is only acceptable on cable TV and the Internet and in movies and magazines, so the pilot diverted the plane, delaying all the passengers and wasting extra fuel, so the nudist could be covered and arrested. This award goes to the pilot. Running out of coffee is a far more worthy cause for diverting a flight.   Source: Associated Press, July 2, 2009

HONORABLE MENTION

On a British Airways flight from London to Jamaica, a British couple admittedly gained membership into the "mile-high club" (more accurately, the six-mile-high club) in the plane's lavatory. Twice. Their sexual acts, coupled with additional disturbances in the cabin when they were refused further drinks, were somehow enough to divert the entire flight to Bermuda and have the pair escorted off the plane in handcuffs—no, not the pink fuzzy type.   Source: *Bermuda Sun*, December 2005

TITANIC AWARD

LEAST REASSURING MAINTENANCE PRACTICE

WINNER

Nepal Airlines

Nepal Airlines was having technical trouble with one of its two Boeing 757s. Eventually, the airline announced that it had corrected the problem by sacrificing two goats to appease the Hindu god of sky protection, Akash Bhairab. The goats were sacrificed in front of the aircraft, right on the tarmac of Tribhuvan International Airport in Kathmandu.

"The snag in the plane has now been fixed and the aircraft has

Credit: AFP

resumed its flights," said senior airline official Raju K.C., according to a Reuters report.

It may be worth noting that after the ceremony, the plane did complete a successful flight to Hong Kong. Source: Reuters, BBC, September 5, 2007

PERSONAL WORST

WORST LANDING   *Not a fair question. I tell people that judging a flight by a rough landing is like judging a book by a single misplaced punctuation mark. From a pilot's point of view, there is so much that goes into a flight, and to judge everything by the smoothness of a touchdown is unfair. Especially when some landings are intentionally firm, such as those on shorter runways. That's my excuse, anyway, for those times when I bang it on.*

—Patrick Smith, commercial airline pilot, air travel columnist for *Salon*, and author

---

TITANIC AWARD

MAJOR EUROPEAN AIRPORT WITH MOST DELAYS

WINNER
London Heathrow

Q1 2008 was its most impressive quarter, with 42.1 percent of flights delayed an average of 38.8 minutes.

Top 10 runners-up in order: Gatwick, Rome, Paris Charles de Gaulle, Madrid, Dublin, Athens, Frankfurt, Stockholm, Lisbon, Manchester.

Source: *Association of European Airlines Consumer Report*, based on average quarterly ranking of percentage delayed for the most recent year

PERSONAL WORST

WORST AIRLINE *Undoubtedly the late and unlamented Viasa of Venezuela. In the olden days of the late twentieth century, this basket-case airline provided the only really cheap link between the UK and South America. Halfway through a tortuous, 25-hour trip from Heathrow via Paris, Margarita Island, Caracas, and Rio to São Paulo, I contracted the worst food poisoning I have ever experienced. Since all the "meals" I consumed in that time were provided by the airline, I can pin the blame squarely on Viasa. In a gratifying bit of travel karma, this useless airline went bust shortly afterward.*

—Simon Calder, travel editor for the *Independent* and TV travel host for the BBC

TITANIC AWARD

MOST BREAST-AVERSE AIRLINE

WINNER

Emily, a 27-year-old New Mexico native who took an ironically named Freedom Airlines flight (operated by Delta Airlines) between Burlington and New York City, filed a claim that she was kicked off her flight for breast-feeding her baby daughter. It's not like she was walking around the plane topless while carrying her baby about. She said she had a window seat in the next-to-last row and was further shielded from public view by her husband, who was seated between her and the aisle. She noted that she was being discreet—no part of her breast was showing. Breast-feeding is actually recommended on flights, as it helps the baby's ears deal with altitude change and comforts the baby also—as far as other passengers are concerned, it's a nice alternative to screaming. The airline disagreed with Emily's assessment, the case went to court six months later (during which time 900 people participated in nurse-ins to show support for Emily at 40 airports across the country), and the Vermont Human Rights Commission found that Freedom Airlines was guilty of discrimination.

Source: MSNBC, November 16, 2006

PERSONAL WORST

WORST AIRLINE *Cubana, Yucatan to Havana. All the overheard bins flew open. Some of the seats came loose. And the flight crew—like, eight of them for a 22-seater—kept coming in and out of the cockpit like it was a swingers party in there.*

—Chantal Martineau, freelance travel, food, and drink writer, and Travel Channel program host

---

TITANIC AWARD

AIRPORT WITH WORST SHOPPING (OF 50 BIGGEST)

WINNER

LAX (Los Angeles)

AFRICA/MIDDLE EAST WINNER: Dubai

ASIA WINNER: Bangkok

EUROPE WINNER: Paris Charles de Gaulle

LATIN AMERICA WINNER: Mexico City

NORTH AMERICA WINNER: LAX (Los Angeles)

PACIFIC WINNER: Sydney

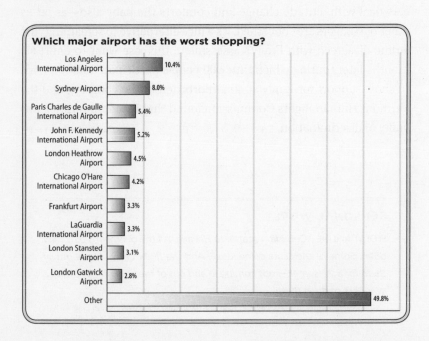

Which major airport has the worst shopping?

Airport	Percentage
Los Angeles International Airport	10.4%
Sydney Airport	8.0%
Paris Charles de Gaulle International Airport	5.4%
John F. Kennedy International Airport	5.2%
London Heathrow Airport	4.5%
Chicago O'Hare International Airport	4.2%
Frankfurt Airport	3.3%
LaGuardia International Airport	3.3%
London Stansted Airport	3.1%
London Gatwick Airport	2.8%
Other	49.8%

TITANIC AWARD

MOST CREATIVE PILOT EXCUSE FOR FAILING A DRUG TEST

WINNER

A helicopter pilot (previously with the New York Police Department) was fired in 2006 for testing positive for cocaine. How did that cocaine get into the pilot? He said it was from performing oral sex on his cocaine-using girlfriend.

Source: *New York Daily News*, April 8, 2009

PERSONAL WORST

WORST AIRLINE SECURITY PROCEDURES *Montenegro Airlines. At Podgorica Airport, I checked my bag and went to the gate, which was just a set of glass doors opening onto the tarmac. I watched as the baggage handlers unloaded all of the bags halfway between the plane and the gate. On the walk outside to the air stairs, I had to stop at the pile and point: "That's my bag; now load it onto the plane." Not reassuring.*

—Alexander Basek, Best Deals reporter for *Travel + Leisure*
and coauthor of Fodor's Prague guidebook

TITANIC AWARD

MOST DEMANDING TAXI

WINNER

Shandong Airlines

Taking off shoes at security, limited luggage, extra fees . . . think airlines are asking a lot of you these days? Maybe you don't have it so bad. Passengers on a Chinese Shandong Airlines flight were asked to get out and push the 20-ton plane about 800 meters (half a mile) when it broke down shortly after landing. (The airport staff gave it a try first but weren't able to get it near the gate without the additional help.) It took them two hours. Still, they were able to keep a positive outlook. "Thank God it was only a 20-ton medium-size plane," said one of the airport workers. Probably won't be long before airlines ask us to roll down the window and flap our arms. Source: *Daily Mail/Telegraph*, September 27, 2008

Credit: Europics/Alloverpress

TITANIC AWARD

MOST EXPENSIVE FLIGHT PER MILE

WINNER

A Delhi-based man named Bahadur bought an old Airbus 300 to offer weekly sessions in which any of the 1 billion Indians who had never flown before could sit on a genuine (though disabled) airliner, listen to pilot announcements ("We are about to begin our descent into Delhi"), and be served by flight attendants. Said one customer (who paid the equivalent of about $4), "I see planes passing all day long over my roof. I had to try out the experience."

The experience of sitting on an airplane and not leaving the ground is far more realistic than the passengers may realize. Few air travelers haven't experienced delays on the tarmac. Bahadur just needs to change his pilot announcements to: "Sorry for the delay. We're still waiting for the go-ahead from the control tower—apparently there are a lot of flights backed up trying to land in Chicago, and we're just waiting for a new departure slot. But we expect that anytime now. Meanwhile, sit back and relax, and we'll do everything we can to make this part of your journey as pleasant as possible." Source: *Times* (London), September 30, 2007

PERSONAL WORST

WORST AIRLINE *Bangladesh Biman. Passengers blowing snot on floor; one pulled out a camp stove ready to make tea.*

—Larry Habegger, cofounder and editor of Travelers' Tales publishing

---

TITANIC AWARD

MOST OVERVALUED LOST LUGGAGE

WINNER

We've all encountered overpriced flights. Seems like US Airways got a taste of questionable pricing when they managed to lose the Xbox of a 21-year-old Yale University student named Jesse (it was reportedly stolen from his luggage). There may only be a government liability of $3,300 per bag, but Jesse filed a lawsuit for more than $1 million—$1,700 for the gaming consol, $1 million for damages. Good luck.

Source: Associated Press, March 11, 2009

PERSONAL WORST

WORST FLIGHT ATTENDANTS *Qantas. They really don't give a shit.*

—Peter Moore, Australian travel writer and author
of several books, including *Vroom with a View*

MOST HATED AIRPORT
(OF 50 BIGGEST)

WINNER

London Heathrow

AFRICA/MIDDLE EAST WINNER: Dubai

ASIA WINNER: Bangkok

EUROPE WINNER: Heathrow

LATIN AMERICA WINNER: Mexico City

NORTH AMERICA WINNER: LAX (Los Angeles)

PACIFIC WINNER: Sydney

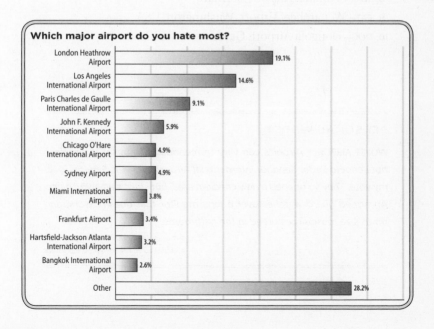

Which major airport do you hate most?

Airport	%
London Heathrow Airport	19.1%
Los Angeles International Airport	14.6%
Paris Charles de Gaulle International Airport	9.1%
John F. Kennedy International Airport	5.9%
Chicago O'Hare International Airport	4.9%
Sydney Airport	4.9%
Miami International Airport	3.8%
Frankfurt Airport	3.4%
Hartsfield-Jackson Atlanta International Airport	3.2%
Bangkok International Airport	2.6%
Other	28.2%

TITANIC AWARD

MOST UNFORTUNATE IATA AIRPORT CODES

WINNER

DOH

1. DOH—Doha Airport, Qatar
2. FAT—Fresno Yosemite Airport, California, USA
3. POO—Pocos de Caldas Airport, Brazil
4. DIK—Dickinson Airport, North Dakota, USA
5. NOB—Nosara Beach Airport, Costa Rica
6. BUM—Butler Airport, Missouri, USA
7. PEE—Perm Airport, Russia
8. SEX—Sembach Airport, Germany
9. EAT—Wenatchee Airport, Washington, USA
10. DOG—Dongola Airport, Qatar

PERSONAL WORST

WORST AIRPORT *Airports can vary tremendously terminal to terminal, but Leopold Sedar Senghor International Airport, in Dakar, Senegal, gets my vote. They've opened a new check-in area, but still it's an awful place. An armed guard watches over a lone monitor that doesn't work, and moth-size mosquitoes breed in the bathrooms.*

—Patrick Smith, commercial airline pilot,
air travel columnist for *Salon*, and author

TITANIC AWARD

NARROWEST COMMERCIAL PLANE SEAT

WINNER
Northwest Airlines

Northwest Airlines can lay claim to the world's narrowest sea (on board their Saab 340), measuring in at a hip-crunching 16 inches. By comparison, the industry average for economy seats is closer to 17.5 inches. And a few economy seats are as wide as 19 inches. So if you find yourself flying on Northwest's Saab 340, you'll be pleased to know that in this case, it's not you getting bigger. Source: SeatGuru.com, July 1, 2009

PERSONAL WORST

WORST AIRPORT LINK *No place in the world rips off airport commuters more than the sweet New Jersey Transit to Newark's airport—that is,* if *you're coming in from New York City. It's a plain ol' commuter train (not much place for your bags) but charges $15 per person for the two-stop, 24-minute trip. That might be okay if it weren't triple the cost if you get off a stop before or after the airport. Meanwhile, New Jersey Transit's hour-long ride to the airport from Trenton, clear across Jersey? Yeah, it's $9.25. Probably just payback for New York stealing Liberty Island.*

—Robert Reid, Lonely Planet's U.S. spokesperson and travel editor

TITANIC AWARD

SPECIFIC FLIGHTS WITH MOST DELAYS

WINNER

ExpressJet

The FAA knows exactly which flights have the most delays and prints a list of them every quarter. To make the list, the flight needs to be at least 15 minutes late 70 percent of the time.

Looking at the most recent year of statistics available, ExpressJet had the most flights that achieved this impressive status, with 29 flight routes that were at least 15 minutes late at least 70 percent of the time. Close behind were American and Comair, each with 26 flight routes on the list.

Most impressive, perhaps, is Comair's Q3 record (July–September 2008) for its Minneapolis to JFK flight, which was delayed by 15 minutes or more 62 out of 63 times, for a single-quarter record 98.4 percent delayed. (The industry average is close to 20 percent.)

Source: Bureau of Transportation Statistics (most recent available year of FAA reports: 2007–2008)

PERSONAL WORST

WORST AIRLINE *Air Pakistan: duct tape holding together seats, cockroaches in the aisles.*

—Pauline Frommer, publisher and founder of Pauline Frommer's Travel Guides

---

TITANIC AWARD

SUSPENSION FROM AIRLINE AWARDS LIST

WINNERS
Azerbaijan Airlines and FlyGlobespan

Skytrax ranks airlines on a one- to five-star system for quality standards. Last year, six airlines received the top score of five stars. Air Koryo (the national airline of the Democratic People's Republic of Korea) stood alone at the bottom of the ranking as the lone one-star recipient.

But two have the dubious distinction of being suspended from Skytrax's list: Azerbaijan Airlines and FlyGlobespan. According to Skytrax, "Suspending an airline from Star Ranking may relate to concerns about safety, or where wide variations of product/service inconsistency and reliability make ranking inaccurate."

When you visit FlyGlobespan's website, it has the words "award winning" right under the logo. Wonder if it's counting this as an award.

Source: Skytrax, July 30, 2009

PERSONAL WORST

WORST AIRPORT *Well, it used to be JFK, but that seems to have improved a bit, so I guess I'd have to say Heathrow.*

—Martin Dunford, former publisher of the Rough Guides series

TITANIC AWARD

U.S. AIRLINES WITH MOST CANCELED FLIGHTS

WINNER

Comair

In the most recent year statistics were available, 4.5 percent of Comair's flights were canceled (the national average is 2 percent).

HONORABLE MENTIONS

- JetBlue Airways (3.2 percent of flights canceled)
- United Airlines (3.2 percent of flights canceled)

Source: U.S. Department of Transportation (2007–2008)

PERSONAL WORST

WORST AIRLINE *A tie. Between easyJet and Ryanair. Forget the come-on Internet fares. The real sticker shock comes if you try to check in a bag, even if you pay the extra £5 ($8) to do it. It's a total scam, and neither airline excels in essential full disclosure. So . . . if you're homeless, a fugitive from justice, or just entered the witness protection program, these are the airlines for you, because I presume you will board with nothing more than what you're wearing.*

—Peter Greenberg, investigative travel reporter and producer, served as correspondent for ABC's *Good Morning America* and travel editor for NBC's *Today* show

---

EDITOR'S
CHOICE

TITANIC AWARD

WORST ADDITIONAL IN-FLIGHT FEE

WINNER

FlyGlobespan

No-frills means no-frills. The budget carrier FlyGlobespan sparked a row after William Davidson, a 77-year-old wheelchair passenger traveling from Edinburgh to Alicante, was hit with a £30 ($49) fee for—get this—using his wheelchair. The fee was, according to the airline, justified because the passenger did not inform the airline of the wheelchair use ahead of time.

Source: *Edinburgh Evening News*, April 8, 2005

HONORABLE MENTION

Jet2, a no-frills carrier that flies out of Leeds, Manchester, Belfast, Blackpool, and Edinburgh, set a new standard in baggage fees when it charged Mick Skee, a double amputee, $25 to bring his prosthetic legs with him. Okay, on the one hand they were his spare set of legs. But they were made especially for use in the warm climate of Majorca, where he was headed. Besides, wheelchairs are transported free of charge (FlyGlobespan excluded).

Source: *Daily Mail*, November 4, 2008

PERSONAL WORST

WORST AIRLINE POLICY *Charging for water. You can't take your own through security, yet SAS, Ryanair, and countless others charge $4 for it. Pure trap-and-gouge.*

—Jason Cochran, travel writer, guidebook author, and blogger

TITANIC AWARD

WORST AIRLINE MEAL

WINNER
Estonian Air

Marco 't Hart, editor of AirlineMeals.net, has collected more than 20,000 photos of airline meals from about 600 airlines in every flight class imaginable. They were sent to him by thousands of travelers with a shared interest in photographing and critiquing airline food. The following meals were sent in by such travelers and selected by Marco as the worst he had ever seen:

Used with permission of Marco 't Hart

1. ESTONIAN AIR

WHERE: Served on a Tallinn to Copenhagen flight.

TASTER'S COMMENTS: What was in the meal? Very good question! Starter: cold rice with a few peas, sweet corn, and olive skin. Main course: I believe it was cold Baltic herring (those three pieces of gray, slimy things on the left), potato salad (recycled, I think), lettuce (left by the snails as being inedible), a piece of tomato (for color), a bread roll (warm on arrival, but overdone in microwave, so solid within a few minutes). Dessert: able to break this stodgy, doughy thing into pieces, but no flavor at all, so not sure what it was supposed to be.

TASTER: Allen

Used with permission of Marco 't Hart

2. AIR BOTSWANA

WHERE: Johannesburg to Gaborone

TASTER'S COMMENTS: Meat something with vegetable something. This is a trick question . . . right? The drink was some fluorescent green soda.

TASTER: Gina

Used with permission of Marco 't Hart

3. AEROFLOT

WHERE: Moscow to Malta

TASTER'S COMMENTS: The worst I've had from Aeroflot. The salmon was the same age as my grandma . . . lunch was poor and not fresh. HORRIBLE!

TASTER: Andrei

Used with permission of Marco 't Hart

4. ALITALIA

WHERE: Düsseldorf to Milan

TASTER'S COMMENTS: It's supposed to be aubergine, I guess. Coffee came right out of the engine, undrinkable.

TASTER: John

5. UKRAINE INTERNATIONAL

WHERE: Kiev to London

TASTER'S COMMENTS: The most striking thing about this meal was the lurid yellow color of the omelet. Decidedly unnatural, but perhaps this was the caterer's attempt to support the Orange Revolution in Kiev. Sausage was pure plastic, so I didn't touch it—and I wasn't sure why it was split down the middle . . . to reveal its meat-free content perhaps?

TASTER: Jess

PERSONAL WORST

WORST AIRLINE *Ryanair. Every airport they fly into is an hour or two from the city you're actually trying to reach, they've got one of the ugliest sites on the Internet, and they charge extra for everything (like online check-in and "payment handling").*

—Sarah Schlichter, editor of IndependentTraveler.com

TITANIC AWARD

WORST AIRLINE PAINT SCHEMES

WINNER

Germanwings

Credit: Timo Breidenstein

Nothing quite sums up the spirit of Berlin (or a competent airline staff) like a giant orange dog wearing sunglasses.

Credit: Sam Chui

Nokair

Look, it's a bird, it's a plane ... no, it's a plird. Or maybe a Blane. We get the whole bird/plane reference, but this one doesn't quite seem to work.

Credit: Stewart Andrew

SkyEurope Airlines

Nice use of windows for eyes—that's not at all creepy.

Swiss Air

Extraordinary. They managed to cram every national stereotype onto one fuselage.

Hapag-Lloyd Express (HLX)

Ah, the elusive flamingo-taxi combo. It conjures up a powerful mix of stuck in traffic with the meter running while standing on one leg in an uncomfortable position.

Sky Airlines

Impressive how Eve's breasts are censored by the windows.

RUDEST FLIGHT ATTENDANTS (OF TOP 50 CARRIERS)

WINNER
Tie: American and United Airlines

AFRICA/MIDDLE EAST WINNER: Turkish Airlines

ASIA WINNER: Shanghai Airlines

EUROPE WINNER: British Airways

LATIN AMERICA WINNER: n/a*

NORTH AMERICA WINNER: American and United Airlines

PACIFIC WINNER: Air New Zealand

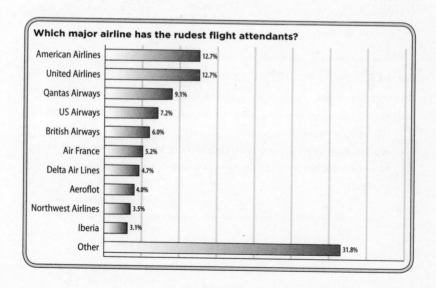

Which major airline has the rudest flight attendants?

Airline	Percentage
American Airlines	12.7%
United Airlines	12.7%
Qantas Airways	9.1%
US Airways	7.2%
British Airways	6.0%
Air France	5.2%
Delta Air Lines	4.7%
Aeroflot	4.0%
Northwest Airlines	3.5%
Iberia	3.1%
Other	31.8%

*Note: Not enough votes in this region to indicate a conclusive winner.

TITANIC AWARD

WORST AIRLINE SAFETY ANNOUNCEMENT

WINNER
Vueling Airlines

Passengers boarding a Vueling Airlines flight in Madrid, Spain, couldn't help but notice that all but three rows of seats on one side of the plane had been taken out of service. While they pondered how half of the plane had come to be deemed unfit for passengers, a captain's announcement tried to put them at ease: "We have a safety problem with the door at the front. Don't worry, it's only a safety problem."

Source: Reuters, June 11, 2006

PERSONAL WORST

WORST AIRPORT *Miami International if I am coming off an international flight. I have missed more internal connections there than anywhere, simply because of the sheer number of people going through immigration. If you arrive when a Caribbean, Latin American, Central American, or Mexican flight has arrived, you have time to get married and divorced in the line.*

—Richard Quest, host of *CNN Business Traveller*

EDITOR'S
CHOICE

WORST AIRLINE TICKETING PRACTICE

WINNER
Ryanair

When Ulrika Örtegren-Kärjenmäki tried to pass security controls at London Stansted Airport, the bar code on her boarding pass failed to register and she was told to go to the Ryanair customer service desk. The problem? Turns out her name was too long for the boarding pass and contained the Swedish letters ö and ä. The queue was so long at the information desk that Örtegren-Kärjenmäki and her daughter missed their flight, had to buy new tickets, and spent an extra night in a hotel in London. Ulrika Örtegren-Kärjenmäki's name cost her $756.

Source: *Dagens Nyheter* (Swedish newspaper), September 20, 2008

PERSONAL WORST

WORST AIRPORT SECURITY *Nepal's domestic terminal. As elsewhere in South Asia, "ladies" are searched separately, behind a curtain. The young female officer didn't look up from filing her nails. "Do you have big knife?" she asked. No. "Do you have bomb?" No. "You may go." Well, okay, then, if you say so . . .*

—Catherine Watson, travel writer and former travel editor of the *Minneapolis Star Tribune*

TITANIC AWARD

WORST AIRPORT NAMES

WINNER

Moron

1. Moron Airport, Mongolia
2. Useless Loop Airport, Australia
3. Dang Airport, Nepal
4. Brest Airport, France
5. Mafia Airport, Tanzania
6. Pratt Airport, Kansas, USA
7. Wee Waa Airport, Australia
8. Woodie Woodie Airport, Australia
9. Flin Flon Airport, Canada
10. Asbestos Hill Airport, Canada

PERSONAL WORST

WORST FIRST-WORLD AIRPORT   *Terrible third-world airports are no great achievement; LAX and Charles de Gaulle compete for the title of worst in the first world.*

—Tony Wheeler, founder of Lonely Planet

TITANIC AWARD

WORST AIRPORT SIGN

WINNER

Minneapolis–St. Paul International Airport

This sign sends approximately 25,000 people to the wrong terminal each year. "Lindbergh? Humphrey? Quick, honey, what does it say on our tickets? Crap, it doesn't say anything!" Minneapolis–St. Paul has two terminals side by side, and you've only got seconds to figure out which one you're flying out of before the turnoff. With no easy connecting road, that means a lot of stress and/or missed flights. The Metropolitan Airport Commission, during an eight-day stretch, measured 600 people who picked the wrong airport. Make that Land of 10,000 Lakes and 25,000 Pissed-Off Travelers.

Source: Associated Press, July 20, 2009

Credit: AP/Jim Mone

TITANIC AWARD

WORST BAGGAGE SCREENER

WINNER

As if there's not enough to think about as you go through a security screening (shoes off, belt off, laptop out, liquids in Baggies, watch off, dump loose change, hold your boarding pass), you might also want to keep an eye on the baggage screeners. Pythias, a 48-year-old TSA screener at Newark Liberty Airport, was doing a bit of collecting. When he was arrested, police found the mother lode of gadgets in his home: iPods, GPS devices, cameras, jewelry, laptops, even professional video equipment. It was CNN that did him in—not its news reporting but when he stole a CNN camera and a search pulled up someone attempting to sell it on eBay. (HBO also had a $47,000 camera stolen at the airport turn up on eBay.) After CNN contacted the police, a trap was set, and Pythias was caught. In total, he admitted he nicked between $200,000 and $400,000 worth of travelers' belongings.

Source: WABC New York, October 8, 2008; New Jersey Department of Justice news report, March 19, 2009

PERSONAL WORST

WORST AIRPORT *Near Lake Kariba, Zimbabwe. After issuing my boarding pass, the agent jogged out to the runway to chase away monkeys. A few minutes later, I swear I saw him giving flag signals to the plane.*

—Christopher Reynolds, travel writer for the *Los Angeles Times*

TITANIC AWARD

WORST BALANCED PLANE

WINNER

Thomas Cook

Passengers in Mallorca balked when British charter airline Thomas Cook asked them to sit at the back of the front-heavy plane (a rear luggage door had jammed, so bags could only be loaded into the front of the plane). Especially since those disembarking from the flight down were kissing the ground, crying, and warning others not to get on the plane after the worst flight of their lives. In total, 71 passengers refused to board the flight back to Newcastle and were forced to pay for new tickets on a different flight. One passenger, Dave Charlton, paid £600 ($975) for his family to rebook tickets. "It's just not worth the risk," he told Sky News. "All we asked was that they fix it. We just wanted a plane that would stay level without us being used as ballast." No, that doesn't seem like too much to ask.

Source: Sky News, *Daily Mail*, June 23, 2009

EDITOR'S CHOICE

WORST AIRLINE NAMES

WINNER
Enimex

1. **ENIMEX AIRLINES.** It may be based in Tallinn, Estonia, but it sounds like a Mexican enema at 30,000 feet.

2. **WIZZ AIR.** Low-cost Hungarian airline. Seems to put too much emphasis on being able to urinate while flying.

3. **KRASAIR.** Short for Krasnoyarsk Airlines, based in Russia. Kras is just a little too close to crash. The airline shut down in 2008.

4. **TED.** A budget, even lower service version of United—now defunct.

5. **BMIBABY.** Low-cost, hard-to-be-taken-seriously-with-a-name-like-that subsidiary of BMI (British Midland Airways).

6. **AER LINGUS.** Phlegmy-sounding Irish national carrier.

7. **CANJET.** A low-cost chartered airline based in Nova Scotia. Sounds just a little too positive . . . conjures up thoughts of Can'tJet.

8. **SONG.** Delta's low-cost, brand with a name better suited for an mp3 player.

9. **VALUJET/AIRTRAN.** Hard to say which name is worse: ValuJet sounds like a supermarket with wings. AirTran sounds like a third-world charter flight.

10. **TANGO.** The discount airline spin-off of Air Canada. Nothing like the image of Canadians dancing tango to make you want to fly.

WORST CARRY-ON SOUVENIR

WINNER

Holy Water

Even on Mistral Air, a special Vatican-chartered flight, pilgrims were getting no special treatment. Several attempted to bring small bottles of holy water on board—water samples collected at Our Lady of Lourdes Cathedral. They were denied by security officials at the Tarbes-Lourdes-Pyrenees International Airport in southern France. The pilgrim-passengers protested, as they had waited in long lines to get the holy water, but they had to decide between dumping the holy souvenir and getting on the plane. Source: Italian news agency Apcom and Associated Press, September 29, 2007

EDITOR'S
CHOICE

TITANIC AWARD

SCARIEST AIRPORT TO FLY INTO (OF 50 BIGGEST)

WINNER

Hong Kong Kai Tak*

AFRICA/MIDDLE EAST WINNER: Dubai

ASIA WINNER: Hong Kong Kai Tak

EUROPE WINNER: London Heathrow

LATIN AMERICA WINNER: Mexico City

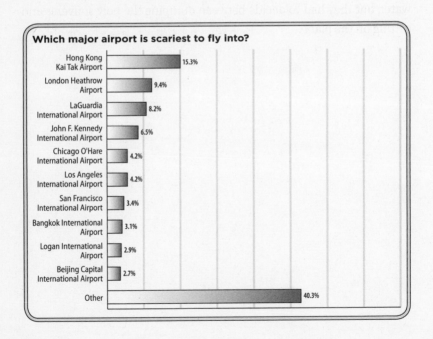

Which major airport is scariest to fly into?

Airport	Percent
Hong Kong Kai Tak Airport	15.3%
London Heathrow Airport	9.4%
LaGuardia International Airport	8.2%
John F. Kennedy International Airport	6.5%
Chicago O'Hare International Airport	4.2%
Los Angeles International Airport	4.2%
San Francisco International Airport	3.4%
Bangkok International Airport	3.1%
Logan International Airport	2.9%
Beijing Capital International Airport	2.7%
Other	40.3%

NORTH AMERICA WINNER: LaGuardia

PACIFIC WINNER: Sydney

*Note: Hong Kong Kai Tak closed in 1998. At that time, there was only one runway, which required a steep bank turn at the last minute before landing. The others, for the most part, are ranked here because of a combination of traffic congestion and poor weather.

PERSONAL WORST

WORST IN-FLIGHT MEAL   *I hate it on short, overnight flights from the U.S. East Coast to London when they wake you two hours before landing for "breakfast" and then just give you a muffin that has a sell-by date of June 2019 and a cup of lukewarm dirty water that they laughingly call coffee.*

—Will Hide, London-based freelance travel writer with a weekly column in the *Times*

TITANIC AWARD

WORST CHECK-IN MISUNDERSTANDING

WINNER

With all the new security regulations and airlines already treating us like cargo, it's not too hard to imagine a 78-year-old Swedish woman misunderstanding a request while checking in at Stockholm's Arlanda Airport en route to Germany. She was directed to an unmanned baggage conveyor for her luggage. Instead, she placed herself on the conveyor belt, and before anyone could act, she was whisked away and tumbled down to the luggage collection area. She was met by surprised airport personnel who helped her catch her flight on time.

Source: *Upsala Nya Tidning*, August 26, 2008

WORST CONCEPT FOR PASSENGER SEATING

WINNERS

Ryanair/Spring

Standing room only doesn't sound so bad ... at a rock concert. But on a flight? Enter low-cost Irish airline Ryanair and Chinese airline Spring. They're both looking to reduce costs (or make sardines jealous) by giving passengers a bar stool with a seat belt. No food, no water, no service—like a bus. They're currently seeking permission for the proposal. Ryanair CEO Michael O'Leary has, according to the *Sun*, spoken with Boeing about designing a jet with standing room. Spring estimates it could pack in as many as 50 percent more passengers and cut costs by 20 percent by using standing room. A Ryanair spokesman said, "If they approve it, we'll be doing it."

Source: *Daily Mail,* July 6, 2009

TITANIC AWARD

WORST DAMAGE NEGLECT

WINNER
SriLankan Airlines

While taxiing at Heathrow Airport, a Sri Lankan Airlines pilot drove his A340 into a parked British Airways 747, clipping five feet of the wing off the SriLankan jet and delaying takeoff 24 hours.

Passengers were put in hotels and told they'd be put on a new plane. When the passengers returned the following day for their new flight to Colombo, they were surprised to see that the same plane was being used. And the damaged wingtip had not been fixed.

The airline insisted that the wingtip was for fuel efficiency and would not affect the safety of the plane. Nonetheless, several passengers revolted, and seven were let off before the plane departed.

Source: *Daily Mail*, November 4, 2007

WORST DEPLANEMENT

WINNER

Why do first-class passengers get to exit the plane first? Here's one reason: impatience. After a flight from New York touched down in Georgetown, Guyana, a first-class Guyanese passenger on a Delta flight, identified as Satyanand, was forced to wait for economy-class passengers to exit the plane. This allegedly intoxicated passenger took matters into his own hands and made his own getaway: out the emergency exit and down the chute. At least he was paying attention during the safety lecture.

Source: Associated Press, July 7, 2008

TITANIC AWARD

WORST DISCRETION, AIRLINE VERSION

WINNER
Southwest Airlines

When a curvaceous college student (and Hooters employee) named Kyla tried to board her summer Southwest Airlines flight from San Diego to Tucson, an airline employee informed her that her short skirt and tight top were too provocative for American airspace and denied her entry.

With a few sartorial modifications, she was allowed to board her flight, but the damage was done. The Internet was abuzz with the story, and she appeared on national TV (in the same outfit—which didn't seem too provocative for the networks) to explain her tale. Though Southwest may fail to see the irony, it is the very same airline that once made its own flight attendants wear hot pants. Source: MSNBC, September 11, 2007

UGLIEST FLIGHT ATTENDANT OUTFITS (OF TOP 50 CARRIERS)

TITANIC SURVEY

WINNER

Qantas Airways

AFRICA/MIDDLE EAST WINNER: Emirates Airline

ASIA WINNER: Malaysia Airlines

EUROPE WINNER: British Airways

LATIN AMERICA WINNER: n/a

NORTH AMERICA WINNER: United Airlines

PACIFIC WINNER: Air New Zealand

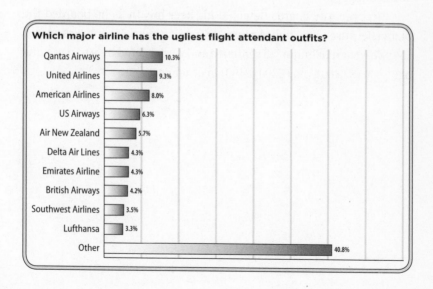

Which major airline has the ugliest flight attendant outfits?

Airline	Percentage
Qantas Airways	10.3%
United Airlines	9.3%
American Airlines	8.0%
US Airways	6.3%
Air New Zealand	5.7%
Delta Air Lines	4.3%
Emirates Airline	4.3%
British Airways	4.2%
Southwest Airlines	3.5%
Lufthansa	3.3%
Other	40.8%

TITANIC AWARD

WORST EXCUSE FOR ATTEMPTING TO FLY DRUNK

WINNER

An American Airlines pilot named Joseph was arrested at Heathrow Airport for attempting to fly a 204-passenger-full Boeing 777 from London to Chicago with twice the legal limit of alcohol coursing through his veins.

Captain Joe, a decorated former U.S. Air Force pilot, had what he thought was a legitimate excuse: The British beer he had been drinking was too strong. That is, it was stronger than the American beer he was accustomed to.

Alert security guards detected his beer breath as he boarded the plane. Because of his unbesmirched 40-year record, Joseph was spared the two-year maximum jail sentence and was ordered only to pay a fine of £1,500 ($2,400), plus £300 ($490) in other costs. Source: *Daily Mail*, July 17, 2009

WORST FIRST-CLASS
SEATMATE

WINNER

Paul, a 54-year-old businessman who flies more than 200,000 miles a year, was enjoying his first-class British Airways flight from Delhi to England. But when a woman in her seventies died in coach, she became his seatmate. And she was joined by her grieving daughter. "It was terrifying," he told the *Times*. "I put my earplugs in but couldn't get away from the fact that there was a woman wailing at the top of her voice just yards away. It was a really intense, primal sound." Then there's the issue of—as Paul put it—having a decaying body on a plane at room temperature for five hours. He voiced a complaint, presumably about the discomfort of being seated beside a corpse and the value of his $4,500 ticket. "Get over it," BA told him. Compensation? Nope. And it didn't end when the plane landed. He had to remain in his seat for another hour for police and a coroner to sign off on the death scene. He voiced a complaint, presumably about the discomfort of being seated beside a corpse and the value of his $4,500 ticket. "Get over it," BA told him. Clearly his suffering doesn't begin to rank with the woman's loss, but you might wonder if this is where that often-hyped customer service might come into play. Nope, it didn't. Source: *Sunday Times*, March 18, 2007

TITANIC AWARD

WORST FLIGHT FOR PEOPLE WITH ALLERGIES

WINNER
Pet Airways

Welcome to Pet Airways, the first airline that specifically caters to passengers with pets. No, they won't place your children in the cargo hold, but they're not keeping your pets there either. Instead, the new pet-sensitive airline puts the "pawsengers" in private, secure carriers in a special section of the main cabin of a cleared-out Beech 1900 passenger plane. There, they can receive pre- and post-flight potty breaks and get a little mid-flight loving as well. Nice for pets; not so great for people with allergies.   Source: Associated Press, July 15, 2009

WORST IN-FLIGHT CHAT-UP

WINNER

During a flight from St. Petersburg, Russia, to Turkey, a woman declined the advances of an inebriated Russian man trying to chat her up. Instead of accepting defeat, he punched her in the face. A fight ensued with two other drunken men on the Russian flight, and the melee forced the plane to return to St. Petersburg, where the men were fined "dozens of thousands of dollars," according to police—adding, you might say, injury to insult. Source: Reuters, July 13, 2007; Russian News and Information Agency, July 2007

TITANIC AWARD

WORST AIRLINE FOOD (OF TOP 50 CARRIERS)

WINNER

American Airlines

AFRICA/MIDDLE EAST WINNER: EgyptAir

ASIA WINNER: Air China

EUROPE WINNER: Aeroflot

LATIN AMERICA WINNER: n/a

NORTH AMERICA WINNER: American Airlines

PACIFIC WINNER: Qantas Airways

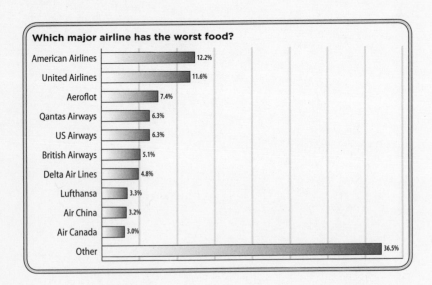

Which major airline has the worst food?

Airline	Percentage
American Airlines	12.2%
United Airlines	11.6%
Aeroflot	7.4%
Qantas Airways	6.3%
US Airways	6.3%
British Airways	5.1%
Delta Air Lines	4.8%
Lufthansa	3.3%
Air China	3.2%
Air Canada	3.0%
Other	36.5%

WORST IN-FLIGHT PRAYER

WINNER

The last thing airline passengers want to hear is a pilot crying and calling out for God in mid-flight. On January 28, 2008, that's exactly what happened on Air Canada flight 848 from Toronto to London.

"He specifically said he wanted to talk to God," Sean Finucane, one of the 149 passengers on board the flight, told Canadian broadcaster CBC. "He was yelling loudly but didn't sound intoxicated."

The copilot suffered a nervous breakdown and had to be dragged kicking and screaming out of the cockpit, bound, and placed in an empty economy-class seat for the remainder of the flight.

Source: *London Evening Standard*, January 30, 2008

TITANIC AWARD

WORST LEGROOM

WINNER
Qantas Airways

Finally a seat guaranteed to give you venous thrombosis on a domestic flight—that is, if you can get your legs in at all. You might have to have them flattened and folded first. Perhaps Qantas is now offering this service.

Credit: Sam Kindler

TITANIC AWARD

WORST BATHROOM BLOCKING

WINNER

SkyWest Airlines

If there's one light on a plane you don't want to malfunction, it's the light in the plane's only bathroom, which was enough of a perceived problem for the pilot to render it off-limits during a SkyWest Airlines flight, which didn't leave the passengers much to do except cross their legs and pray. That is, except for one especially acute urinator who, according to the *Salt Lake Tribune*, "had two really big beers." He reported that he "had no choice" but to pee into an airsickness bag. "I really had to go. I kept asking three or four times, 'may I use the bathroom?' She kept telling me no. The fourth time I asked, we were in final descent, which was her excuse," he said. A clever solution? Perhaps, but the flight attendant and pilot didn't think so. The pilot called the police upon landing in Salt Lake. The airline later issued an apology and gave the passenger a travel voucher.

Source: *Salt Lake Tribune*/Associated Press, March 17, 2007

TITANIC AWARD

WORST NAPPING

WINNER

For passengers, it can be a luxury to fall asleep on a plane—sitting up-right with less legroom than most of us had in utero. Different standards should apply for pilots. We'd like to think that the people flying the plane will remain awake. On the other hand, it's rather impressive that both the captain and the first officer managed to fall asleep at the same time, while staring at all those blinking lights, with information from the control tower blaring in their ears, and on just a 30-minute commercial flight (from Honolulu to Hilo) on February 13, 2008. It's probably safe to assume their 40 passengers weren't all that impressed. When an air traffic controller instructed the flight to change radio frequencies, there was no response. It wasn't until about 30 miles southeast of Hilo that the pilot called the controller, who asked if they were experiencing an emergency. Nope, they were just sleeping (they later admitted). They reversed course and landed without incident. The Federal Aviation Administration handed the pilot and copilot 60-day and 45-day suspensions respectively. Source: *Honolulu Star Bulletin*, August 4, 2009

TITANIC AWARD

WORST AIRLINE OVERALL (OF TOP 50 CARRIERS)

WINNER

United Airlines

AFRICA/MIDDLE EAST WINNER: n/a

ASIA WINNER: China Southern Airlines

EUROPE WINNER: Aeroflot

LATIN AMERICA WINNER: AeroMexico

NORTH AMERICA WINNER: United Airlines

PACIFIC WINNER: Qantas Airways

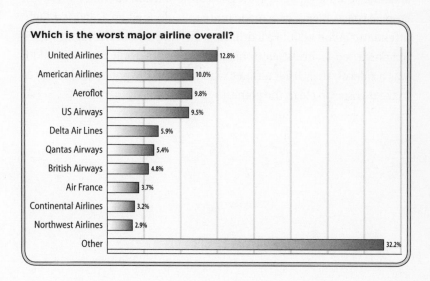

Which is the worst major airline overall?

Airline	Percentage
United Airlines	12.8%
American Airlines	10.0%
Aeroflot	9.8%
US Airways	9.5%
Delta Air Lines	5.9%
Qantas Airways	5.4%
British Airways	4.8%
Air France	3.7%
Continental Airlines	3.2%
Northwest Airlines	2.9%
Other	32.2%

TITANIC AWARD

WORST NEW SAFETY REGULATION

WINNER

SkyWest Airlines

Joe Sharkey of the *New York Times* got a firsthand taste of SkyWest Airlines enforcement of a new safety procedure. Prior to takeoff, the flight attendant announced that passengers could not place any items in the seat-back pockets—all because (she said) of a new safety regulation from the Federal Aviation Association. So the magazine and the safety instruction manual currently there are okay, but don't even think of stashing your newspaper, a few postcards, or a book in that convenient storage space. It was even made more ridiculous when a SkyWest flight attendant "enforced it like a drill sergeant throughout the flight." When Sharkey tried to investigate this new regulation, only SkyWest said it was a safety issue. Other airlines who adopted the policy said it was to make it easier to clean the plane. Source: *New York Times*, September 7, 2009

WORST PET SAFETY RECORD

WINNER
Continental Airlines

Out of the 32 pets that died during U.S. flights in 2007, 12 flew Continental Airlines. That's 37.5 percent of all deaths occurring on one airline!

HONORABLE MENTIONS

Alaska Airlines had the most pet injuries (seven). Delta lost the most pets (seven)—which represents 46.7 percent of the total lost pets on U.S. flights.

Source: *Air Travel Consumer Report*, U.S. Department of Transportation (most recent year of available statistics: 2007–2008)

TITANIC AWARD

WORST SEAT ASSIGNMENT

WINNER

JetBlue

Gokhan, a JetBlue passenger, was en route from New York to Angeles when an off-duty flight attendant took his seat and he was ordered by the captain to stand up or "hang out in the bathroom" for the duration of the flight. It's not pleasant to stand for five hours or sit in a JetBlue bathroom for that long, but few among us wouldn't endure it for $2 million, which is the amount he sued the airline for.

Apparently there was a slight conflict over who got the seat. The off-duty JetBlue employee originally wanted the jump seat in the cockpit, but changed her mind and wanted a normal seat. Gokhan had a standby travel voucher. In terms of seat-assignment value, for those of you keeping score, apparently an employee ID card beats a travel voucher.

Note: This could be a double winner for Most Excessive Lawsuit *and* Worst Seat Assignment.

Source: Associated Press, May 16, 2008

WORST SEATMATE

WINNER

Warning: What economy-class lacks in comfort, it may make up for in unwanted adventure. On a recent Southwest Airlines flight heading from Oakland to Las Vegas, Darius, a 21-year-old man, exposed himself to the woman seated beside him. She screamed. He punched her for screaming. Then he removed his clothes. The pilot turned around and landed back in Oakland, where a team of police officers subdued him. The woman was taken to the hospital. So much for the friendly skies.

Source: *San Francisco Chronicle*, August 21, 2009

TITANIC AWARD

WORST TOILET MALFUNCTION

WINNER
Continental Airlines

Quick: What do you call a transatlantic flight from Amsterdam to Newark with a backed-up toilet spilling human excrement down the aisle for seven hours? Continental Airlines (or perhaps Incontinental Airlines is more appropriate) called it "poor conditions." Probably not the words passenger Collin Brock would have used. He felt "physically abused and neglected," he told Seattle's KING-TV in his home state. The flight was diverted to Shannon, Ireland, to fix the problem. But after the extra stop and delay, the sewage flooding developed again when the plane took off. The reported culprit was a latex glove someone had tried to flush down the loo. Continental apologized to its customers and issued vouchers.

Source: MSNBC.com

TITANIC AWARD

WORST TOILET MISS

WINNER

A 28-year-old named Jerome was sentenced to three weeks in jail after pleading guilty to urinating on a fellow passenger, a 66-year-old woman. The victim was watching an in-flight movie en route from Los Angeles to Honolulu when Jerome, who'd had a few too many drinks, stood up and began relieving himself on her. An agent from the Bureau of Alcohol, Tobacco, Firearms and Explosives was seated two rows behind the woman and backed up her statement. Source: *Honolulu Star Bulletin*, March 24, 2009

TITANIC AWARD

WORST UPGRADE ATTEMPT

WINNER

Bert, a German banker on a Delta flight between Berlin and New York, decided he didn't like his seat in coach. So, doing something we've all considered, he got up and moved to an empty seat in first class.

Bert refused to go back to his economy seat after repeated requests by flight attendants. An altercation between him and one of the attendants led to a scuffle that left the flight attendant pushed to the floor.

The captain diverted the flight and landed in Manchester, where Bert was arrested.

Later, in the court hearing, first officer Douglas Smith was quoted as saying, "[The passenger said] he would pay for an upgrade and would 'die' if he returned to economy class." Bert, I think we can all relate.

Source: *Manchester Evening News*, March 6, 2007

TITANIC AWARD

WORST IN-FLIGHT MAGAZINE

WINNER
Ryanair

AFRICA/MIDDLE EAST WINNER: Turkish Airlines

ASIA WINNER: Air India

EUROPE WINNER: Ryanair

LATIN AMERICA WINNER: Aerolineas Argentinas

NORTH AMERICA WINNER: US Airways

PACIFIC WINNER: Qantas Airways

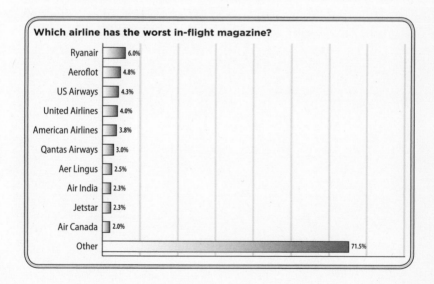

Which airline has the worst in-flight magazine?

Airline	Percentage
Ryanair	6.0%
Aeroflot	4.8%
US Airways	4.3%
United Airlines	4.0%
American Airlines	3.8%
Qantas Airways	3.0%
Aer Lingus	2.5%
Air India	2.3%
Jetstar	2.3%
Air Canada	2.0%
Other	71.5%

TITANIC AWARD

WORST DUTY-FREE DISPOSAL, CUSTOMER VERSION

WINNER

Anti-terrorist measures don't always fit with anti-consumption measures. Rather than surrender a new bottle of vodka at a security checkpoint while switching planes in Germany's Airport Nürnberg, a 64-year-old German (on his way home from a holiday in Egypt) decided to chug it. After downing a liter, he was understandably unable to stand. A doctor was summoned, and he was sent to the hospital, where he nearly died from alcohol poisoning. That's one way to extend a vacation.

Source: Associated Press, December 12, 2007

PERSONAL WORSTS
FLIGHTS

Late 1980s, New Delhi to London. Eight-hour delay, followed by a quick spin around the airport and landing with an escort—a small fire truck with a single hose. We were moved to a hotel, returned 12 hours later to the airport only to find ourselves stuck in an AC-frozen waiting room with no open food facilities; after another four-hour delay, the passengers rioted.

—Jane Wooldridge, travel editor of the *Miami Herald*

★

I was flying over the Amazon in a small plane with five passengers and—KABOOM—there's this atomic concussion. I look out the window and five feet of the wing is missing. Then we start losing altitude. We all think we're going to die. So I mentally say good-bye to my family and friends. Fifteen minutes go by and we still haven't crashed yet, but I've said my good-byes to everyone. So I start thinking that this is going to hurt. I dwell on that for a while. The plane will explode and I'm going to catch on fire. Then out of nowhere appears a tiny airfield and we manage to plop down on it. Turns out it's a secret military base that wasn't expecting us. We're met by lots of people pointing guns and detained. And there's no cell phone coverage here. And they don't know what has happened. At that point, neither did we. Our theory was that another plane higher up had exploded and we hit their debris. What actually happened was that we were hit by another, much larger 737, and that plane tragically went down and 154 people died. We found out several hours later.

—Joe Sharkey, travel columnist for the *New York Times*

★

Toss up. It might be the Air Rangoon flight from Kuala Lumpur on a 1952 DC-something with chickens, goats, and a pilot who was probably used to driving a school bus. The plane was making spastic jerks all over the sky, then finished off with a near-death landing. Or maybe it was a private-jet flight that got caught in a thunderstorm. We were hit by lightning a few times, then the lights went out and the plane dropped a few thousand feet. My fingerprints are still in the armrest. —Keith Bellows, editor in chief of *National Geographic Traveler*

★

Atlanta to Maui, Delta Airlines. Connecting flight into Atlanta was delayed on arrival, so I missed breakfast. Boarded my Maui-bound flight starving, and ordered two box meals after takeoff. Flight attendant handed 'em over, but at that time Delta only took cash—no credit cards. Attendant wouldn't budge and swiped the boxes back. Faced with a nine-hour fasting, I stood up and pleaded with her. Three flight attendants rushed me, threatening to turn the plane around, contact federal authorities, and so on. Not a soul spoke to me the rest of the flight. Using the bathroom required escorts. I just wanted a box lunch. —Eddy Patricelli, editor in chief of *Islands* magazine

★

Flying from Bogotá to Puerto Asis in the Amazon basin on a DC-3. It was very old and had propellers. I don't recall the airline. Half the passengers were humans, the other half were chickens. The chickens were scared and trying to fly in their cages as we took off, and all of them literally shit themselves. It smelled really bad. And the plane looked like it was falling apart. I'm not a religious person, but I was praying that day.
—Nori Kunori, Japanese adventurer, travel writer, and professor

★

Riau Airlines. Right after takeoff cockroaches began to emerge from air vents and scurried along the ceiling as if competing in a Formula 1 race. —Dave Lowe, travel writer and author of *Sandwiches Should NEVER Taste Like Cow Crap*

★

Air Fiji before they got their newer, larger planes. Everything was smooth on my puddle-jump ride to Savusavu until we went over the mountain range. We hit turbulence, an alarm went off, the plane dropped, and I had to pound my heart a couple of times to start that sucker back up once we flattened out. When we landed, I not only kissed the ground but made out with it.
—Johnny Jet (aka John E. DiScala), founder/editor of JohnnyJet.com

★

A Cubana Airlines internal flight with chickens in the overhead compartments and livestock in the aisle. On the final approach to Havana I thought I was going to die (from the smell).

—Rory MacLean, travel writer and author of several books, including *Stalin's Nose*

★

I took a charter flight from Darwin, Australia, to a lodge in Arnhem Land. The plane turned out to be a two-seater. It was just the pilot—who looked awfully young—and me in the jump seat. Halfway into the flight, he asked me to pull out the map. He peered at it and flew on. A little later he asked me if that area below looked like the marked spot on the map. At that moment it dawned on me that the guy had never been to where we were going before. Then I started to panic and wondered if he'd ever flown solo before; he assured me he had. Now, those who are familiar with my sense of misdirection would never ask me to navigate, but we somehow managed to locate the airstrip. To top off this surreal adventure, after we landed I had to get out and help park the plane by pushing it under some trees.

—Norie Quintos, senior editor at *National Geographic Traveler*

★

Arolineas Sosa is one of the few carriers that fly from the Honduras mainland to the Bay Islands. They have no websites, published schedules, or seat assignments. Everyone tosses their bag onto the back row of seats when they get on the plane, and after takeoff, the pilot (who was sitting within kicking distance) opened up a newspaper.

—Grant Martin, editor of Gadling.com

PART 2

SURFACE TRANSPORT

OVERLAND AND SEA TRAVEL

Anywhere is walking distance, if you've got the time.

—STEVEN WRIGHT

At one point in our history, going overland used to be the only form of transport. The oldest pair of shoes (found in the "stolen from Egypt" section of the British Museum) date from 1500 BCE and are made from papyrus. The first stone road may be the Via Appia (circa 300 BCE), an ancient Roman creation linking Rome with Brindisi (early hotels even sprang up alongside it to house travelers). Similarly, cruising hasn't always been about zipping around in tropical circles on a ship the size of Greenland while force-feeding yourself at midnight with enough calories to power a small Prussian army.

About 50 years ago, overland travel achieved cult status with the Hippie Trail—a popular road trip that grew out of the 1960s the same way just about everything else did at the time: with a search for spiritual enlightenment. Or, at any rate, drug-induced enlightenment. Or, at any rate, drugs. Throw in sex, rock 'n' roll, adventure, and a VW bus, and what self-respecting flower child could possibly refuse? The basic plan was to start in Europe and make your way toward Kathmandu.

The allure of stumbling along old roads is unpredictability itself. You literally bump into and rub up against other people in a way that never happens on an airplane (except maybe on Ryanair). Hence, more room for unexpected misadventures.

Today, overland travel applies to almost anything except flying and long ocean crossings. It can mean seniors taking a cruise to Cancun or a converted army vehicle taking more adventurous travelers across Africa or South America. But, as with other modes of transport, the better we get at making these modes faster and more comfortable, the higher we raise expectations and set up the likelihood of grievances. (Though several ground-transport companies, such as Greyhound and British Rail, are doing their best to reverse these expectations by consistently providing dilapidated equipment and frequent delays.)

DIRTIEST CRUISE SHIP

WINNER

The Peace Boat (aka TSS *Oceanic*)

What happens if you let the Centers for Disease Control and Prevention (CDC) snoop around cruise ships? Well, they'll probably find some bacteria that shouldn't be there. And they did. In fact, they did more than snoop around. They investigated (2007–2009) and filed a report. Not surprisingly, some boats weren't up to snuff. A score below 85 is considered by the CDC to be a fail. The Peace Boat (aka TSS *Oceanic*) nailed a 73. Among the complaints: the sneeze shields were too high because of the depth of the tray slides, and there were trays of sliced cold cuts and cheese that were tested at 46 to 48.6 degrees Fahrenheit.

HONORABLE MENTIONS

- *PRIDE OF ALOHA.* Sample complaint: The backflow prevention device on the soap dispenser was leaking. Score: 78.

- MV *CLIPPER PACIFIC.* Sample complaint: There were numerous potable water connections throughout the vessel that were not fitted with backflow prevention devices. Score: 84.

- *AMADEA.* Sample complaint: The deck at the starboard bar side, beneath the coffee counter, was heavily soiled with black tile glue and dirt debris, and there were electrical cords stuck to the deck in the debris, which made cleaning difficult. Score: 84.

- *CELEBRITY INFINITY.* Sample complaint: A food employee was observed tasting food with his finger. Score: 84.

TITANIC AWARD

LAMEST BUS HIJACKING

WINNER

After hiding in a bus's on-board restroom, an armed man jumped out and forced the tour-bus driver at gunpoint to drive him to the Downtown Disney area. According to the sheriff's office, no one was injured and the bus hijacker made it to the Disney area just fine. Of course, if he couldn't afford the bus fare, how was he planning to pay the entrance fee?

Source: Associated Press, October 25, 2008

PERSONAL WORST

WORST ROADS   *Romania is part of the EU, but don't tell that to the narrow roads and their potholes the size of Buicks. After a week's worth of driving across Transylvania, I felt lucky getting out of there without a scrape—or a collision with a racing Dacia in the wrong lane on a blind curve. The best part, though, is watching the occasional horse cart, sweeping triumphantly off an ancient path on a hillside, across the highway, and up over other hills and out of sight. They have no use for the roads.*

—Robert Reid, Lonely Planet's U.S. spokesperson and travel editor

COUNTRY WITH THE WORST BUSES

WINNER

India

AFRICA/MIDDLE EAST WINNER: Egypt
ASIA WINNER: India
EUROPE WINNER: United Kingdom
LATIN AMERICA WINNER: Mexico
NORTH AMERICA WINNER: United States
PACIFIC WINNER: Australia

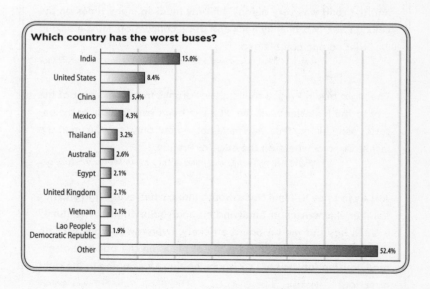

Which country has the worst buses?

Country	Percentage
India	15.0%
United States	8.4%
China	5.4%
Mexico	4.3%
Thailand	3.2%
Australia	2.6%
Egypt	2.1%
United Kingdom	2.1%
Vietnam	2.1%
Lao People's Democratic Republic	1.9%
Other	52.4%

PERSONAL WORSTS
BUSES

On the island of Flores, Indonesia. Apparently the locals don't travel much, and their stomachs are very weak. Every bus ride we took people were shouting "plastique!" to get a shopping bag to throw up into. If there was no plastique, the vomit went out the window, onto the floor, or onto an unfortunate seatmate.

—Tim Leffel, author of *The World's Cheapest Destinations*
and editor of *Perceptive Travel*

★

The 30-hour bus ride from Golmud, China, to Lhasa, Tibet. There was not an actual road, it was very cold (due to the roughly 5,000-meter [3-mile] mountain passes), and the bus driver was blasting the same clangy music tape over and over again while folks chain-smoked cigarettes throughout the ride.

—Sean Keener, founder of BootsnAll.com

★

Kathmandu to the Indian border. I got a seat in the back of the bus, and the road was very bumpy. I hit my head so many times on the ceiling I nearly broke my neck and got a concussion. Most amazing was that no one complained.

—Nori Kunori, Japanese adventurer, travel writer, and professor

★

The night bus in Prague that shuttles drunks from the center of the city to the hinterlands of the city. I've been vomited on, had cigarettes ashed in my face, and have passed out only to wake up at the last stop, somewhere on the edge of Prague.

—David Farley, travel writer and author of *An Irreverent Curiosity*

★

A risky journey in Tamil Nadu, South India, when every sign and bus number was written in Tamil and no one spoke English. Eventually a small boy put me on board a rickety, overcrowded bus with no windows, where I was given pride of place on the boiling hot engine housing for the next six hours, hoping I was going in the right direction.   —Melissa Shales, chairperson of the British Guild of Travel Writers

★

Laos. The bumpiest 11 hours of my life, on roads so excruciatingly potholed we averaged 12 miles per hour, were on a bus from Luang Prabang up to Luang Nam Tha in the northern hill-tribe country. It took my lumbar spine six months to recover.

—Wendy Perrin, consumer news editor and columnist for *Condé Nast Traveler*

★

The harrowing drive through the mountains from Jiuzhaigou to Chengdu in Sichuan, China. Extra points for the big bag of fresh yak meat the driver bought at a stop along the road and tossed in the bus aisle. The lower we descended in the mountains, the warmer it got, the greater the stench became, and the more yak blood streamed over the bus floor.

—Jim Benning, founder and editor of WorldHum.com

★

Sarajevo to Banja Luka, Republika Srpska, Bosnia and Herzegovina. The bus, a charter, was fine, but I was trapped with a mixed group of authors and poets from the former Yugoslavia—Bosnian, Croat, Serb, and Montenegrin—who were all reading together in Banja Luka that night. The tension, sadness, and resentment in the air was palpable.

—Evan Rail, travel writer

★

Ouagadougou, Burkina Faso, to Coutonou, Benin. They had about 30 percent more seats than reasonable; five seats across rather than four, and rows so tightly bunched your legs couldn't go straight. It took contortions to achieve a seated position. The trip was 14 hours.

—Brook Silva-Braga, travel documentary filmmaker

★

A bus ride on the island of Java. I sat on the roof and was hit in the eye with a low-hanging electrical cable.

—Daniel Hoffer, CEO and cofounder of CouchSurfing.com

TITANIC AWARD

LEAST LUCKY CAR-CRASH SURVIVOR

WINNER

In Nelson, California, a 34-year-old named Jeffrey managed to walk away after his vehicle rolled over. Distracted or disoriented after the accident, he wandered over to some nearby railroad tracks, where he was hit by a passing Amtrak train and killed. Wonder what his horoscope said that morning.

Source: Associated Press/*Sacramento Bee*, May 25, 2009

PERSONAL WORSTS
CAR RENTAL

Avis in the country of Jordan. Seems that cars are rented on "empty" or with very little gas in the tanks . . . with no notice of that local practice. I found out the hard way, 41 kilometers (25 miles) away.
—Randy Petersen, founder of FlyerTalk.com

★

Easily the dude on Hvar, Croatia, who rented me a wrecked Fiat Panda with no reverse gear for the local equivalent of $110 per day. (Pro tip: If you do end up renting a car on Hvar, do not attempt a three-point turn on one of the island's tiny mountain roads.)
—Evan Rail, Czech Republic–based travel writer for the *New York* Times and other publications

---

MOST CROWDED TRAIN

WINNER

There's first class and there's second class, but I don't know what you'd call the seating on this Pakastani train, except perhaps hanging-on-for-dear-life class. These Sunni Muslims are on their way back from the annual three-day Daawat-e-Islami religious congregation in Multan, Pakistan. The good news is that it would have been even more crowded if the railroad hadn't organized an extra 11 trains. Where they stay during the event isn't much more spacious—a tent village on 250 acres that holds 1 million people.

Credit: AP/Khalid Tanveer

TITANIC AWARD

MOST EXPENSIVE MISSED FLIGHT

WINNER

After missing his flight to his friend's bachelor party at Munich's Okto-berfest, a passenger (known only as Dave) decided to take a taxi. The cabdriver, Mick Hogan, thought the request for the 740-mile ride was a joke at first, but he agreed to do it after seeing a wallet full of bills. It took 17 hours and cost Dave £1,950 ($3,170). "[Dave] had tried to find alternative flights but had been unsuccessful," Hogan said. "He was ob-viously in a hurry and told me he had to get to Munich straightaway."

Source: *Daily Telegraph*, October 5, 2008

PERSONAL WORST

WORST OVERLAND KAYAK TRANSPORT   *Gabon. We had an 18-mile portage through the jungle to get from river to lagoon. Unfortunately, the tires on the portage carts I'd brought with us were all punctured within the first 24 hours, which turned a day-and-a-half portage into a three-and-a-half-day portage as we literally dragged the kayaks through the jungle.*

—Jon Bowermaster, *National Geographic* writer, filmmaker, and kayaker

TITANIC AWARD

MOST IRONIC END OF A SAILING ADVENTURE

WINNER

When professional travelers and eco-activists Raoul Surcouf and Richard Spink attempted to make the first carbon-neutral crossing of Greenland's polar ice cap, they set sail from Bristol on a 40-foot boat complete with wind turbine and solar panels. The environmentally friendly adventure was thwarted by an unfriendly environment. Just 400 miles off the coast of Ireland, hurricane-force winds thrashed the boat to destruction. Fortunately, the crew was rescued by a passing ship—an oil tanker with 680,000 barrels of crude on board. Source: *Guardian*, May 6, 2009

PERSONAL WORST

WORST SUBWAY SCHEDULE   *The subway in Rome, the eternal city, closes down earlier than most suburban day-care centers.*

—Spud Hilton, travel editor for the *San Francisco Chronicle*

TITANIC AWARD

COUNTRY WITH THE WORST DRIVERS

WINNER
Italy

AFRICA/MIDDLE EAST WINNER: Egypt
ASIA WINNER: India
EUROPE WINNER: Italy
LATIN AMERICA WINNER: Mexico
NORTH AMERICA WINNER: United States
PACIFIC WINNER: Australia

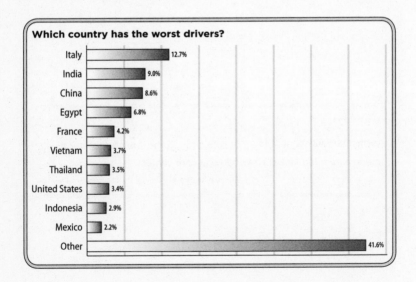

Which country has the worst drivers?

Country	Percentage
Italy	12.7%
India	9.0%
China	8.6%
Egypt	6.8%
France	4.2%
Vietnam	3.7%
Thailand	3.5%
United States	3.4%
Indonesia	2.9%
Mexico	2.2%
Other	41.6%

TITANIC AWARD

MOST QUESTIONABLY HAPPY TRAIN CONDUCTORS

WINNER

Keihin Electric Express Railway

Keihin Electric Express Railway, a Japanese train company, has installed face-scanning machines made by the Omron Corporation to check if their employees are smiling broadly enough to present a good impression. Okao Vision, as it's called, rates the 530 employees daily on a scale of 0 to 100 based on "eye movement, lip curves and wrinkles." At least you know why they're faking that smile. Source: *Mainichi Daily News*, April 7, 2009

PERSONAL WORST

WORST TRAFFIC JAMS   *Bangkok passed the baton on to Manila, but despite competition from Dubai, the place that is way out in front—i.e., completely stationary—is Shanghai.*

—Tony Wheeler, founder of Lonely Planet

TITANIC AWARD

WORST ALLEGED NUDITY

WINNER
TRAX Passengers

It's one thing to get pulled off a train by officials for exhibitionism, but quite another when you were never naked. This is what happened to a woman riding the TRAX light-rail service in Utah. Three fellow commuters thought she was not wearing any pants and reported her for it. She may not have been wearing pants, but she did have on a miniskirt. And if they had lifted up the jacket on her lap, they would have seen it. With some clever investigative work, Utah Transit Authority officers concluded that the passenger was in fact wearing a miniskirt and that it counted as clothing. They allowed her back on the train.

Source: *Salt Lake Tribune*, October 27, 2008

PERSONAL WORST

WORST METRO *Glasgow Underground. Tiny as a dollhouse, loud as a jet, and it only goes around in a circle.*

—Jason Cochran, travel writer, guidebook author, and blogger

COUNTRY WITH WORST HIGHWAYS

WINNER

India

AFRICA/MIDDLE EAST WINNER: Egypt

ASIA WINNER: India

EUROPE WINNER: Russian Federation

LATIN AMERICA WINNER: Mexico

NORTH AMERICA WINNER: United States

PACIFIC WINNER: Australia

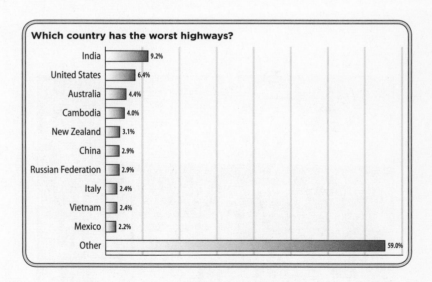

Which country has the worst highways?

Country	%
India	9.2%
United States	6.4%
Australia	4.4%
Cambodia	4.0%
New Zealand	3.1%
China	2.9%
Russian Federation	2.9%
Italy	2.4%
Vietnam	2.4%
Mexico	2.2%
Other	59.0%

TITANIC AWARD

WORST CAR RENTAL NAME

WINNER

Rent-a-Bomb

It's not a front office for Al Qaeda, but at a time when terrorism is still causing panic, it's probably best not to have to mention the bomb you're driving around.

Credit: Ralph Samuelson

TITANIC AWARD

WORST CELLULAR DISTRACTION

WINNER

Credit: AP

Even if you're a multitasking driver, you have to stand in awe of tow-truck driver Nicholas, who, with a car attached to his flatbed, tried texting on one phone while speaking on another. As a result, he must have been steering with his knees while giving the occasional distracted glance to the road. Not surprisingly, this little communications stunt did not end well. He collided with another car, driven by a 68-year-old woman; crashed through a fence; and both vehicles (the tow truck and the car it was carrying) took a plunge into a swimming pool—a far-fetched scene even for a bad Hollywood summer comedy. It was nearly three vehicles in the pool—the motorcycle the tow truck was also carrying flew off just before the truck went into the drink. The first responders were a bit surprised by what they found. "You've got 90 years of service here, and nobody's ever seen anything like this," local fire chief Barry Kobrin told the *Lockport Journal.*

Source: *Lockport Journal*/MSNBC/Associated Press, July 31, 2009

PERSONAL WORSTS
TRAINS

One from Delhi to Bombay that was supposed to be an already grueling 24 hours. It turned into 36 hours, much of the extra 12 hours spent stopped in a nasty station in alcohol-free Gujarat with the train fans turned off and the temperature at around 100 degrees Fahrenheit. —Tim Leffel, author of *The World's Cheapest Destinations* and editor of *Perceptive Travel*

★

On a night train from Krakow to Wroclaw, I was drugged and robbed. Apparently it's a semiregular occurrence on night trains in Poland. The robbers slip a canister of gas into your carriage, knock you out, and rob you. The bar stewards. Luckily it was back in the mid-digital age (2004), so they only made off with a shitty camera and a Discman.

—Benji Lanyado, travel writer for the *Guardian*

WORST CRUISE SHIP NAMES

WINNER

SuperStar Aquarius

Not sure which is worse, the lack of creativity among cruise ship names or the irony. It seems every ship these days has to contain the word *Independence*, *Freedom*, *Celebration*—or a synonym. And exactly how much independence or freedom do you get with a fixed itinerary trapped on board a ship with smaller living conditions and fewer choices than you have at home? Not to mention a population density equivalent to the slums of Bangladesh.

If that third trip to the buffet doesn't get you feeling nauseous, the name of the boat just might. Cunard's ships are all Queens. Princess Cruise Lines has 18 ships with names that end in "Princess." Holland America Line has 15 ships with names that end in "Dam" (*Amsterdam*, *Eurodam*, etc.), and Royal Caribbean has 22 ". . . of the Seas." Carnival uses more distinct names, though about half their ships sound like they come with mind-altering medication: *Elation*, *Ecstasy*, *Fantasy*, *Sensation*, *Fascination*. Then you've got several ships sharing the same names, such as *Jewel*, *Freedom*, *Pride*, and *Dawn*. All in all, a pretty sad selection.

But the worst name? If you include ships out of service, it might be Renaissance Lines' series of eight ships named *R1*, *R2*, *R3* . . . *R8*. Or maybe the *Sally Albatross* (renamed the *Cristal* in 2007). But of those currently in operation, the worst-name distinction would go to Star Cruises for *SuperStar Aquarius*. It sounds like a bad musical—*Jesus Christ Superstar* meets *Hair*. The exact sort of crap show you might expect to find on board.

TITANIC AWARD

WORST DOUBLE-DECKER BUS RIDE

WINNER

Those open-top double-decker buses may be popular with tourists, but outside the inner-city tourist zone (and the UK), think twice before riding up top. In fact, two passengers on the top deck suffered fatal head injuries when such a bus passed under Interstate 57 in Illinois on Route 16. Several people were standing on the upper deck, but only the two tallest tragically hit the overpass.

Source: WGN-TV-AP Chicago, June 1, 2009

PERSONAL WORST

WORST PLACE TO RIDE A BIKE *Trans Amazon. There were many bridges on the verge of collapse that had been abandoned by the government. It was raining all the time, and the runoff often flooded across the road. Sometimes you had to wait for the water to go down, and sometimes you just had to swim—with your bike. One of these instant rivers (not on the map) took 24 hours to cross.*

—Nori Kunori, Japanese adventurer, travel writer, and professor

TITANIC AWARD

WORST ENDING TO A TRAFFIC DISPUTE

WINNER

When a 49-year-old RV driver named Alan was stopped by police after a minor accident in Daly City, California, he became understandably upset when they tried to confiscate his vehicle. He decided to protest by lying down in the middle of the street. While officers tried to persuade him to move out of the way, they thoughtfully placed a squad car in front of him to prevent him from being run over. That is until Kevin came along. He was being chased by police in a high-speed pursuit. He rammed the squad car parked in the street, ran over Alan, then ran over him again while trying to speed away from the scene. Alan was hospitalized and survived; Kevin was caught a few minutes later. And if someone had had a video camera rolling, he or she could have nearly retired off of the footage.

Source: *San Francisco Chronicle*, October 3, 2001

PERSONAL WORST

WORST TAXI RIDE *Nagpur, India, to Madhya Pradesh. Craziest 90-kilometer (56-mile), two-and-a-half-hour drive you will ever do. Everyone is passing, even on blind turns. Huge overloaded trucks, packed buses, tuk-tuks, scooters with entire families, cyclists, free-roaming livestock, dogs, monkeys, street hawkers, beggars, and pedestrians. Technically, there are lanes, but no one seems to stay in them. It's a free-for-all.*

—Johnny Jet (aka John E. DiScala), founder/editor of JohnnyJet.com

TITANIC AWARD

COUNTRY WITH WORST BACK ROADS

WINNER
India

AFRICA/MIDDLE EAST WINNER: Egypt
ASIA WINNER: India
EUROPE WINNER: Ireland
LATIN AMERICA WINNER: Costa Rica
NORTH AMERICA WINNER: United States
PACIFIC WINNER: Australia

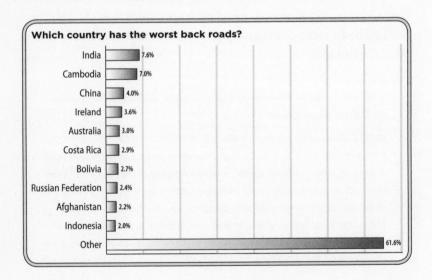

Which country has the worst back roads?

Country	%
India	7.6%
Cambodia	7.0%
China	4.0%
Ireland	3.6%
Australia	3.0%
Costa Rica	2.9%
Bolivia	2.7%
Russian Federation	2.4%
Afghanistan	2.2%
Indonesia	2.0%
Other	61.6%

WORST EXIT FROM A BUS

WINNER

When a 22-year-old soccer fan named Daniel decided to get off the bus, it was still going 60 miles per hour. He and 36 others were just returning from a Manchester United vs. Everton match. A glass had broken on the bus, an argument ensued, and Daniel, who had been drinking and snorting cocaine (according to the autopsy report), was asked to get off the bus at the next stop. He was heard saying, "You want me off the bus, I'll get off here." He then proceeded to leave the bus. Upon his landing on the motorway, a car swerved to avoid him, but the car behind that one wasn't quite as quick.

Source: *Express & Star*, June 27, 2009

PERSONAL WORST

WORST STRETCH OF ROAD FOR A MOTORCYCLE   *If things haven't improved since 2006, any stretch of road in Albania. In just a few short days, I practically destroyed my shocks in the potholes, was attacked by snakes, was shot at, and had the nearest of near misses with a car that came straight at me before flying over a wall. It was like starring in my own Indiana Jones movie.*

—Mike Carter, travel writer for the *Observer* and the *Guardian*, and author of *Uneasy Rider*

EDITOR'S
CHOICE

TITANIC AWARD

WORST FISHING
BY CRUISE SHIP

WINNER

When Royal Caribbean's 90,000-*ton* liner *Jewel of the Seas* pulled into the Canadian port of Saint John, New Brunswick, it appeared as if the captain had done a bit of fishing. There was a 60-foot-long finback whale impaled on the ship's bow, right at the waterline. The awkward catch had taken place somewhere in the Gulf of St. Lawrence.

Source: Associated Press, September 29, 2004

Credit: AP/*The Canadian Press*, Darryl Dyck

COUNTRY WITH WORST TRAINS

WINNER
India

AFRICA/MIDDLE EAST WINNER: Egypt
ASIA WINNER: India
EUROPE WINNER: United Kingdom
LATIN AMERICA WINNER: Bolivia
NORTH AMERICA WINNER: United States
PACIFIC WINNER: Australia

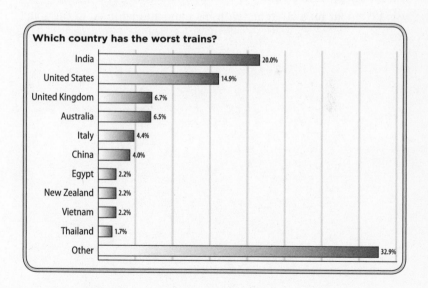

Which country has the worst trains?

Country	Percentage
India	20.0%
United States	14.9%
United Kingdom	6.7%
Australia	6.5%
Italy	4.4%
China	4.0%
Egypt	2.2%
New Zealand	2.2%
Vietnam	2.2%
Thailand	1.7%
Other	32.9%

EDITOR'S CHOICE

WORST ON-TRAIN ACCIDENT

WINNER

TGV Toilet

Little tip: If you drop your cell phone into the toilet of a high-speed French train, do yourself a favor and don't go in after it. One 26-year-old passenger traveling between La Rochelle and Paris simply couldn't resist. While reaching in after it, he set off the powerful flushing mechanism and nearly lost his arm. It was sucked down the hole, and the train had to be stopped for two hours while emergency services cut through the sewage pipes in an effort to save him. According to one witness, he was taken out on a stretcher with his hand still jammed in the toilet bowl. Source: BBC, October 27, 2008

WORST USE OF GPS

WINNER

One Polish driver from the town of Glubczyce had so much confidence in his GPS, he ignored three warnings and followed his dashboard digital map directions right into a lake.

A local police offer explained that the man took a road that was closed a year ago when the area was flooded to make an artificial lake serving as a water reservoir.

The man and his two passengers escaped unharmed from the submerged Mercedes minivan. They were found waiting on its roof for rescue crews to arrive.   Source: Agence France-Presse, October 24, 2008

HONORABLE MENTIONS

Tightest Detour

If only it were an isolated event. A British woman drove her £96,000 ($156,000) Mercedes SL500 into a river, and a Czech driver followed his GPS down an alley too narrow for his truck, which became wedged in place.   Source: *The Register, Leicester Mercury*, March 26, 2007; *Daily Mail*, November 1, 2007

Longest Detour

Yes, GPS devices have been known to steer people onto the wrong road, even into a lake, but usually it doesn't take too long to figure out the gaffe. But it took two Swedish tourists 400 miles to realize they were in the wrong spot. And even then they didn't figure it out for themselves. They had set out for the Italian island of Capri but followed their digital map to the industrial town of Carpi. They didn't realize the mistake until they asked at Carpi's tourist office where they could find the famous Blue Grotto. A Carpi tourism official was amused that the couple could have thought they were on Capri, an island, without having crossed any bridges or boarded a boat. Source: BBC, July 28, 2009

PERSONAL WORSTS
DRIVERS

Republic of Georgia. Most blatant disregard for the rules of the road. And they won't let you use a seat belt—wearing one is an insult to the driver. —Matt Gross, Frugal Traveler columnist for the *New York Times*

★

Having lived in China and Thailand and driven extensively throughout Asia, Europe, America, and Oz, I can honestly say that no one drives as badly as the Italians, apart from the taxi drivers in Istanbul, who are quite simply Satan in a cab.
—Grant Thatcher, publisher of *LUXE City Guides*

★

Have you ever been to South Florida? That stretch of I-95 between Palm Beach and Miami is some of the most dangerous highway in America. Seriously. I wouldn't want to be driving on it after dark. Makes the Daytona 500 look like driving school.
—Christopher Elliott, *National Geographic Traveler's* ombudsman, a nationally syndicated travel columnist, and founder of ConsumerTraveler.com

TITANIC SURVEY

TITANIC AWARD

MOST DIFFICULT CITY TO DRIVE IN (OF TOP 100 CITIES)

WINNER

Cairo, Egypt

AFRICA/MIDDLE EAST WINNER: Cairo, Egypt

ASIA WINNER: Bangkok, Thailand

EUROPE WINNER: London, UK

LATIN AMERICA WINNER: Mexico City, Mexico

NORTH AMERICA WINNER: Los Angeles, California, USA

PACIFIC WINNER: Sydney, Australia

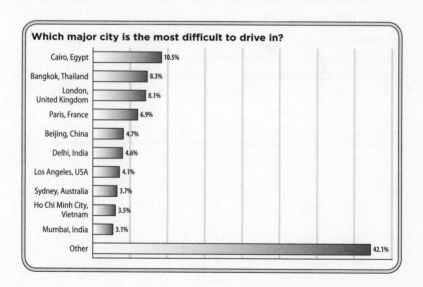

Which major city is the most difficult to drive in?

City	%
Cairo, Egypt	10.5%
Bangkok, Thailand	8.3%
London, United Kingdom	8.1%
Paris, France	6.9%
Beijing, China	4.7%
Delhi, India	4.6%
Los Angeles, USA	4.1%
Sydney, Australia	3.7%
Ho Chi Minh City, Vietnam	3.5%
Mumbai, India	3.1%
Other	42.1%

TITANIC AWARD

WORST WAY TO CHANGE SHIPS MID-CRUISE

WINNER

A man left his four-day cruise to the Bahamas on the Carnival *Sensation* by jumping off while the ship was still at sea. A witness told TKMG-TV in Orlando that she heard the man and a woman arguing. "He threatened to jump, and she said, 'Go ahead,' and he did," the witness explained. He leaped from his stateroom balcony. Once in the water, he had a change of heart and began to yell for help. The U.S. Coast Guard was alerted, but it was a passing Disney cruise ship that picked him up, after 90 minutes of treading water.   Source: *Orlando Sentinel*, September 3, 2009

PERSONAL WORST

WORST WATER FOR KAYAKING   *Anywhere the water temps drop below 35 degrees Fahrenheit . . . as in the Aleutian Islands, where we spent five weeks. And Antarctica, where we recently kayaked the length of the peninsula, 600 miles. Out of the boat in those temps and you've got less than five minutes to live.*

—Jon Bowermaster, *National Geographic* writer, filmmaker, and kayaker

---

TITANIC AWARD

WORST WAY TO PROTEST AIR POLLUTION

WINNER

New York City bus drivers get a lot of mouthing off from their passengers, but 49-year-old Sheila took it to a new low when she bit driver Peter on his arm (right through his jacket, sweater, and thick shirt!). Why? Because she wanted to ride a hybrid bus instead of the more polluting model that picked her up.

"She came on the bus, and she said she waited more than an hour for a hybrid," the driver, 42, told the *New York Daily News*. "I said, 'I'm not in control of what bus is assigned to me.'" Apparently that was enough to trigger her inner Mike Tyson.
Source: *New York Daily News*, January 23, 2009

PERSONAL WORST

WORST CAB EXPERIENCE *Happens at least once a year; shithead NYC cabdrivers who refuse to take you to Brooklyn. Even though* they *probably f*cking live there.*

—Rob Tallia, managing editor of the Not for Tourists guides

TITANIC
SURVEY

TITANIC AWARD

WORST CRUISE LINE

WINNER

Carnival Cruise Line

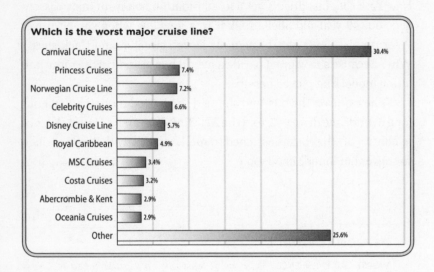

Which is the worst major cruise line?

Cruise Line	Percentage
Carnival Cruise Line	30.4%
Princess Cruises	7.4%
Norwegian Cruise Line	7.2%
Celebrity Cruises	6.6%
Disney Cruise Line	5.7%
Royal Caribbean	4.9%
MSC Cruises	3.4%
Costa Cruises	3.2%
Abercrombie & Kent	2.9%
Oceania Cruises	2.9%
Other	25.6%

TITANIC AWARD

WORST PUBLIC TRANSPORTATION (OF TOP 100 CITIES)

WINNER

Los Angeles, California, USA

AFRICA/MIDDLE EAST WINNER: Cairo, Egypt

ASIA WINNER: Delhi, India

EUROPE WINNER: Athens, Greece

LATIN AMERICA WINNER: Lima, Peru

NORTH AMERICA WINNER: Los Angeles, California, USA

PACIFIC WINNER: Sydney, Australia

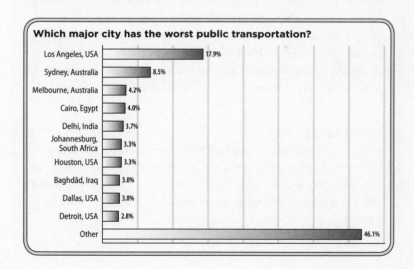

Which major city has the worst public transportation?

City	Percentage
Los Angeles, USA	17.9%
Sydney, Australia	8.5%
Melbourne, Australia	4.2%
Cairo, Egypt	4.0%
Delhi, India	3.7%
Johannesburg, South Africa	3.3%
Houston, USA	3.3%
Baghdâd, Iraq	3.0%
Dallas, USA	3.0%
Detroit, USA	2.8%
Other	46.1%

PERSONAL WORSTS
WATER TRANSPORT

WORST BOAT RIDE

Punta Arenas to Isla Magdalena (aka Penguin Island). The "45--minute" boat ride took three hours. The rough waters of the Strait of Magellan are like a spin cycle. Then when you get there, it reeks of penguin poo.

—Chantal Martineau, freelance travel, food, and drink writer, and Travel Channel program host

★

Mekong River, Thailand to Laos. I was crammed onto a rickety wooden craft that was too small to stand up on. Instead, I huddled on my painful wooden bench for 11 hours and drank my aches away with Beer Lao. —Ian MacKenzie, founder of BraveNewTraveler.com

WORST BOAT SCAM

It was the only one that got me. And just for $1. But I'm still bothered by it. It was on the Corn Islands of Nicaragua. You fly to the big island and take a boat to the little island. I got to the boat dock on the big island and a guy sells me a luggage ticket. Then the boat captain comes over and tells me I need a luggage ticket. I hold mine up for inspection. He looks at it and says that it's not a real ticket. And the guy who sold it to me has disappeared.

—Paul Brady, freelance writer and former editor of Jaunted.com

WORST FERRY RIDE

Melbourne to Hobart, Tasmania. There is not enough Dramamine in the world to stop one from getting sick on this topsy-turvy boat ride through the crazy Bass Strait. They say it is "super-fast," but nothing is super-fast enough when you are vomiting nonstop from 8 p.m. to 7 a.m. —Teresa Rodriguez Williamson, creator of TangoDiva.com

PART 3

HOSPITALITY

In my hotel in Oslo, the chambermaid each morning left me
a packet of something called Bio Tex Blå, a "minipakke for
ferie, hybel og weekend," according to the instructions. I
spent many happy hours sniffing it and experimenting with
it, uncertain whether it was for washing out clothes or
gargling or cleaning the toilet bowl. In the end I decided it
was for washing out clothes—it worked a treat—but for all I
know for the rest of the week everywhere I went in Oslo
people were saying to each other, "You know, that man
smelled like toilet-bowl cleaner."

—BILL BRYSON, *NEITHER HERE NOR THERE*

The word *hotel* comes from the French word *hôte*, or "host." But these days staying in one often feels more like a business transaction than anything to do with being hosted. And with good reason: there are now about 18 million hotel rooms in the world, with around 400,000 new ones added each year.

The largest is the First World Hotel in Malaysia, with more than 6,000 rooms. The oldest hotel currently in operation is Hoshi Ryokan, which opened its doors in Japan in the year 717. The most expensive is the Hotel Martinez in Cannes, France, where the penthouse suite goes for £22,900 ($37,200) a night.

Then there's the parade of weird and unusual places to sleep, from tree hotels to cave hotels to ice hotels to underwater hotels. There are the economical capsule hotels in Japan for those who don't mind cramped plastic spaces. Several hotels have set up shop in renovated structures, like the Jumbo in a 747 by Stockholm's airport. In Bolivia, there's a hotel made of salt. And in New Zealand, hotels are sometimes hobbitlike habitats.

No matter the design of the dwelling, though, the best stories we collect are the ones about hilariously inept management providing existential service.

Now, thanks to the web and some creativity, the hotel is making a return to its roots. Couchsurfing and a few similar organizations are helping connect travelers who need a place to stay with travel-friendly people who don't mind hosting them. And the hosting is genuine—it's done for free.

EDITOR'S CHOICE

TITANIC AWARD

LEAST APPEALING HOTEL NAMES

WINNER

Ufuk

1. Hotel Ufuk (Istanbul, Turkey)

Credit: Peter Wilkins

2. Barf Bed and Breakfast (Barf, England)

Credit: Nancy Hoey

3. Resist Bacteria Hotel (Kashgar, China)

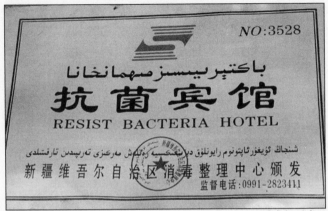

NO:3528

باكتېرىيمسز مهمانخانا

抗 菌 宾 馆

RESIST BACTERIA HOTEL

شىنجاڭ ئۇيغۇر ئاپتونوم رايونلۇق دېزىنفېكسىيە زۇڭلۇش مەركىزى تەربپدىن تارقتىلدى

新疆维吾尔自治区消毒整理中心颁发

监督电话:0991-2823411

Credit: Jenny Andersen

4. Ah Chew (Singapore)
5. Somass Hotel (Port Alberni, Canada)
6. French Lick Resort (Indiana, USA)
7. Arsenic and Old Lace Bed and Breakfast (Arkansas, USA)
8. Black Butte Ranch Resort (Oregon, USA)
9. Wang Thong Hotel (Chiang Raii, Thailand)
10. Elephant Butte Inn (New Mexico, USA)

TITANIC AWARD

TACKIEST HOTEL ARCHITECTURE

WINNER
Dog Bark Park Inn

It's called the Dog Bark Park Inn. Really, what else could you call a 33-foot-high wooden beagle that serves as a hotel? This Idaho hotel also has a bathroom located—wanna guess?—yep, in the dog's ass. But there's a second restroom outside, located in a giant fire hydrant.

It's the brainchild of two chainsaw artists, whose work can be purchased in a shop nearby.

Source: *USA Today*, September 24, 2009

Credit: Idaho Department of Commerce, Division of Tourism

TITANIC AWARD

COUNTRY WITH WORST TOILETS

WINNER

China

AFRICA/MIDDLE EAST WINNER: Egypt

ASIA WINNER: China

EUROPE WINNER: France

LATIN AMERICA WINNER: Mexico

NORTH AMERICA WINNER: n/a

PACIFIC WINNER: n/a

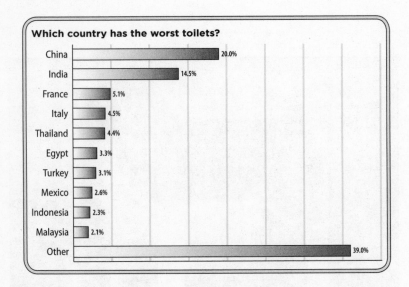

Which country has the worst toilets?

Country	%
China	20.0%
India	14.5%
France	5.1%
Italy	4.5%
Thailand	4.4%
Egypt	3.3%
Turkey	3.1%
Mexico	2.6%
Indonesia	2.3%
Malaysia	2.1%
Other	39.0%

TITANIC AWARD

TACKIEST HOTEL PROMOTION

WINNER

For those looking for a f*cking good deal on a hotel, you might consider the Westin Resort on Aruba. This luxury hotel located on the Dutch island's northern coastline offers couples a discount of $300 if they manage to conceive a child during their vacation. To qualify for the "Conception Credit," the couple must prove that their baby was conceived while they were staying at the hotel. The hotel does not provide staff to sit in the room and watch, but you must obtain a doctor's note confirming that the likely conception date matches the date of your stay.

Source: *Daily Telegraph*, September 14, 2009

HONORABLE MENTION

Venice Beach in Los Angeles already draws an eclectic crowd. The Venice-based Hotel Erwin attempted to capitalize on that by offering a little incentive to would-be guests: a special "Ink & Stay" package for "free-spirited Venice visitors with high pain tolerances only." It came with a $100 tattoo voucher, an ice pack, a bottle of Lubriderm lotion, and a bottle of tequila to ease the pain. If you opted for the house special ("I [heart] hotel Erwin"), you got $500. (Valid for fall 2009 only.)

Source: *Los Angeles Times*, September 6, 2009

TITANIC AWARD

UGLIEST HOTEL

Not only does the 105-story Ryugyong Hotel in North Korea look like a freakish mountain dropped into downtown Pyongyang, but the hotel is deserted. Rather, unfinished. Construction began in 1987 and stopped five years later. Without the prospect of actual tourists coming anytime soon and no money to complete the project, this 3,000-room behemoth will soon be celebrating its eighteenth no-grand opening. What do the locals think? They're probably not allowed to say, but here's one indicator: the building reportedly gets airbrushed out of publicity shots of the city.

Source: *Melbourne Age*, September 7, 2009

Credit: Kyodo via AP Images

TITANIC AWARD

WORST EUROPEAN BUDGET HOTEL CHAIN

WINNER

Formule 1

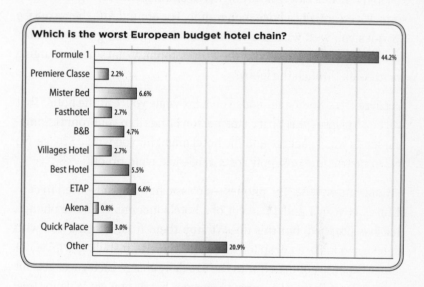

Which is the worst European budget hotel chain?

Chain	%
Formule 1	44.2%
Premiere Classe	2.2%
Mister Bed	6.6%
Fasthotel	2.7%
B&B	4.7%
Villages Hotel	2.7%
Best Hotel	5.5%
ETAP	6.6%
Akena	0.8%
Quick Palace	3.0%
Other	20.9%

TITANIC AWARD

WORST HOTEL RIP-OFFS

WINNER
Resort Fee

1. **RESORT FEE.** This can typically be found at independent, higher-end resorts. It's essentially a huge money grab. For around $10, the resort fee provides you with what the resort should be providing you with anyway: beach towels, access to the fitness room. What's next, charging you to walk through the lobby?

2. **DELIVERY FEES.** Someone sends you a fax while you're at the hotel. That will be $5 please (plus tip if a staff person brings it to your room). Someone sends you a package and the hotel might hit you with a $20 fee. No real infrastructure or supply costs here—just plain rip-off.

3. **PHONE/INTERNET USE.** The phones—a classic hotel rip-off—used to constitute between 1 and 2 percent of a hotel's income. With cell phones, that has dropped, but this doesn't stop them from gouging you with high fees to make a cheap (or free) call. Likewise, installing WiFi is not a huge expense compared with the $15 daily charge each guest gets hit with to use it. Ironically, at many cheaper hotels you get WiFi for free. For most business hotel guests, using the phone and Internet are not optional services. It would be like the hotel charging you extra to use the toilet.

4. **NOT-SO-COMPLIMENTARY WATER.** It looks like the hotel has given you a little gift: a free bottle of water. And it's often not until you've swallowed half the water that you notice the words on the coaster it was sitting on, explaining that it's $6 a bottle.

5. MINIBAR. They know you get the munchies. And they know you're lazy. Which is why your typical hotel minibar has prices jacked up 250 to 500 percent.

6. PARKING FEE. You've arrived by car? Too bad. It's $40 a night to give your car room in the parking garage. "Sure you could leave it on the street," the hotel staff will say, "but we can't take responsibility for any vandalism in this part of the city."

7. BREAKFAST. This depends on the other available options. If you're downtown and there's a Starbucks around the corner, that's one thing, but if you're at a hotel in a remote part of Alaska or on some desolate island, they've got you. You may not want the $30 all-you-can-eat buffet breakfast or the $14 bowl of cornflakes with fruit sprinkled on top, but it's that or starve.

*In consultation with Christopher Elliott, *National Geographic Traveler*'s ombudsman, a nationally syndicated travel columnist, and founder of ConsumerTraveler.com

PERSONAL WORST

WORST HOTEL *I was in Barcelona with my wife, and we just walked along the street looking for a hotel. We spotted one, and I remember thinking how friendly everyone looked. And how many beautiful people seemed to be hanging out in the lobby. It wasn't until after we checked in that I realized it was a whorehouse. When my wife removes her hearing aid to go to sleep, she's nearly deaf, so she couldn't hear a thing. I, on the other hand, could hear everything coming through the walls. The next day I said we had to leave this brothel, and my wife said, "Why? I got a great night's sleep." So we stayed a second night.*

—Howie Shapiro, columnist and former travel editor for the *Philadelphia Inquirer*

TITANIC AWARD

WORST PLACE FOR NICE LIVING CONDITIONS

WINNER
Guantánamo Bay

Prisoners may be locked up without a trial (and tortured), but that doesn't mean Guantánamo is a rough place to stay. Depends on which side of the fence you're living on. In what appears to be Bush-era bad taste, the U.S. military maintains a luxury resort of sorts on this sliver of Cuba. It features air-conditioned suites, surfing, a golf course, and a bowling alley—even a gift shop with T-shirts that read, "The Taliban Towers at Guantánamo Bay, the Caribbean's Newest 5-Star Resort."

Source: *Daily Mail*, May 4, 2008

PERSONAL WORST

WORST HOTEL   *I arrived at 3 a.m. on Christmas Eve in Meiktila, Myanmar, and all the private hotels were full. I didn't want to stay at a military one, so I lingered at a lakeside guesthouse run by a family. After a minute or two of foot shuffling, the staff told me to wait and cleared a tiny broom closet, put in a single bed with a thin mattress, and sprayed and sprayed and sprayed for bugs. "Five dollars. No free breakfast though." I had to keep the door open all night for the fumes. It was ugly and cramped: a windowless box, with spiders immune to bug spray. But I was happy to have it.*

—Robert Reid, Lonely Planet's U.S. spokesperson and travel editor

TITANIC AWARD

WORST NORTH AMERICAN BUDGET HOTEL CHAIN

WINNER

Super 8 Hotels

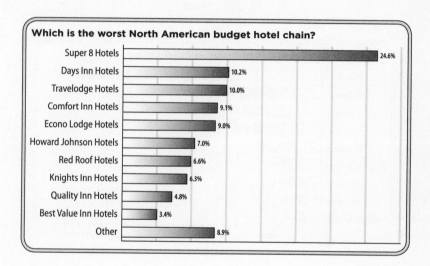

Which is the worst North American budget hotel chain?

Hotel	%
Super 8 Hotels	24.6%
Days Inn Hotels	10.2%
Travelodge Hotels	10.0%
Comfort Inn Hotels	9.1%
Econo Lodge Hotels	9.0%
Howard Johnson Hotels	7.0%
Red Roof Hotels	6.6%
Knights Inn Hotels	6.3%
Quality Inn Hotels	4.8%
Best Value Inn Hotels	3.4%
Other	8.9%

PERSONAL WORST

WORST HOSTEL *Laos. My girlfriend and I were stopped for the night (after our horrendous boat ride) and ended up at the rattiest hostel imaginable. Our bedsheets featured colorful dolphins, which helped the suspicious stains to blend in. Also, the hostel rules were spray-painted on the wall. Classy.*

—Ian MacKenzie, editor of BraveNewTraveler.com

TITANIC AWARD

WORST MAJOR ALL-INCLUSIVE HOTEL CHAIN

WINNER

Club Med

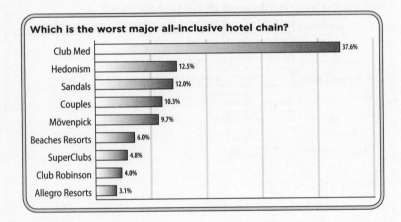

Which is the worst major all-inclusive hotel chain?

Club Med	37.6%
Hedonism	12.5%
Sandals	12.0%
Couples	10.3%
Mövenpick	9.7%
Beaches Resorts	6.0%
SuperClubs	4.8%
Club Robinson	4.0%
Allegro Resorts	3.1%

PERSONAL WORST

WORST HOTEL ROOM *On a 1998 bus tour around Iran, I landed in a cinder-block box in the town of Tabas. Vermin. Spiders. Open loft above the pit toilet, allowing full sharing of sounds and smells from the adjacent pit used by an aged couple next door. Nearby lay the spot where two U.S. aircraft crashed in a failed 1980 hostage-rescue attempt. Cost for one night: $10.*

—Christopher Reynolds, travel writer for the *Los Angeles Times*

EDITOR'S
CHOICE

WORST PLACE TO SLEEP

WINNER

A man decided to sleep off a hangover by taking a nap on the railroad tracks outside of the Swedish town of Borås. He was woken by a train as it hit him in the head. Not a great way to come out of a nice slumber, but the man only sustained minor injuries. The train's driver feared the worst and called the police. When the police arrived, on the side of the tracks they found a sleeping man with a head wound. "He had woken up when the train came, raised his head, and hit it on a metal object on the train. Then he went back to sleep," police officer Sven Persson told TT. Well, of course, what else do you do after you get hit by a train?

Source: TT Swedish News Service, August 9, 2009

PERSONAL WORST

WORST HOTEL   *In Kyaing Tong, Myanmar. It wasn't the trickle of the cold shower in the courtyard. Nor was it the 90 minutes of electricity we got in the evening. It was because the front desk actively tried to sabotage my ability to check out. They'd just disappear. And it's not like you can leave the key and some cash on the desk and go. They had our travel documents. By not being there, they kept us from leaving.*

—Matt Gross, Frugal Traveler columnist for the *New York Times*

TITANIC
SURVEY

TITANIC AWARD

WORST MAJOR LUXURY HOTEL CHAIN

WINNER

Best Western Hotels

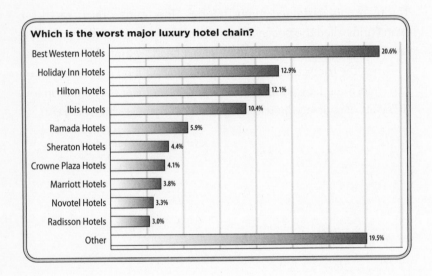

Which is the worst major luxury hotel chain?

Hotel	Percentage
Best Western Hotels	20.6%
Holiday Inn Hotels	12.9%
Hilton Hotels	12.1%
Ibis Hotels	10.4%
Ramada Hotels	5.9%
Sheraton Hotels	4.4%
Crowne Plaza Hotels	4.1%
Marriott Hotels	3.8%
Novotel Hotels	3.3%
Radisson Hotels	3.0%
Other	19.5%

PERSONAL WORSTS
TOILETS

In Mali I asked where the toilet was . . . they pointed outside. There is a lot of outside in Mali. Huts and then sand as far as you could see. And they didn't go inside the huts. So everywhere was the toilet. I was just supposed to wander out into the sand and find a spot in between everyone else's shit and go. With everyone watching. And you know everyone wants to see how the white guy goes to the toilet.

—Robert Young Pelton, filmmaker, speaker, and author of several books, including *The World's Most Dangerous Places*

★

The Throne of Terror, built at an archaeological dig near Lake Petexbatun, Guatemala. Archaeologists are not biologists and constructed the two-holer over an existing vertical cave populated by bats. Visitors are obliged to deal with the common travelers' ailment while angry bats swoop and dive about in a maelstrom of rage.

—Tim Cahill, adventure travel writer, humorist, and author of many books, including *Lost in My Own Backyard*

★

Seoul. It was essentially a trough. For women! You straddled it—it was pretty low—and tried to miss your underwear. I thought it couldn't get any worse until the old lady behind me rested her elbow on my back for support.

—Chantal Martineau, freelance travel, food, and drink writer, and Travel Channel program host

★

Three words that strike fear into the heart of even the most seasoned traveler: Albanian gas station.

—Alexander Basek, Best Deals reporter for *Travel + Leisure* and coauthor of Fodor's *Prague* guidebook

★

The public toilet in Tepelene, Albania. An underground bunker with a floor covered in shit. People simply stood on the stairs leading down and took aim. —Peter Moore, Australian travel writer and author of several books, including *Vroom with a View*

★

Trans-Siberian train going west. No one cleaned it for days. Lots of people got drunk on the train, which led to barfing and shitting all over. After more than four days, it was not pretty.

—Sean Keener, founder of BootsnAll.com

★

No contest. In a bar in a village in central Romania they had an outside toilet up some steps. When you entered, you saw that the toilet was just a very large hole in the floor over a deep pit of sewage about six feet below you. The floor was very slippery, as one can imagine, and the hole easily big enough to fall through. No one would even know you were gone. I have nightmares about it to this day. —Mike Carter, travel writer for the *Observer* and the *Guardian*, and author of *Uneasy Rider*

★

Amur Highway, Siberia. Most of hinterland Russia is a de facto toilet for car travelers; with vast wilderness available, why place effort into concentrating such unpleasantries? However, the very few petrol stations along the only east-west road in Russia (thousands of mostly unpaved, ungraded, and treacherous miles) have wooden outhouses that have never in history been cleaned. In the Siberian summer, when the mosquitoes and flies grow to be as big as birds, anyone who enters one of these dilapidated shacks exits quickly, often screaming, with arms waving about the head.

—Charles Veley, quite possibly the world's most traveled person, having been to 709 of the world's 757 various countries, territories, autonomous regions, enclaves, geographically separated island groups, major states, and provinces

★

Darchen in Tibet. Australians talk of "long drop" outhouses. This was the opposite: a vertical mountain of shit, a long climb to the top.

—Tony Wheeler, founder of Lonely Planet

★

Believe it or not: a public toilet in downtown Portland, Maine. It was like someone let a pack of methed-up children loose on a poo piñata—every conceivable surface was covered. It would've taken a CSI cleanup crew weeks to fully sterilize it, although simply burning it to the ground would've been best. —Mike Richard, Vagabondish.com

★

Too many nasty ones to pick a definitive worst, since I've spent a lot of time in Asia. But for my wife, who was with me on my first long trip, it would be the one in Nagarkot, Nepal, where she had to go down two flights of steps to an outhouse, fill up a bucket to flush the squat toilet, then repeat the process all night while coping with a terrible case of the runs.

—Tim Leffel, author of *The World's Cheapest Destinations*
and editor of *Perceptive Travel*

★

The toilet on the China Railways train from Golmud to Xining looked like a holding pen for baboons with spastic sphincters.

—Jeff Greenwald, director of Ethical Traveler, travel writer, performer, and author of several books, including *Size of the World*

PART 4

FOOD AND DRINK

The food here is terrible, and the portions are too small.

—WOODY ALLEN

We are told to open our minds (and mouths) and try new things when we travel. What happens after we ingest these morsels is sometimes a rather sordid tale. But not withstanding any gastrointestinal dilemmas, the culinary experience can be one of the most enriching of any trip.

Restaurants were first mentioned in the Islamic world in the tenth century. And much like a franchise of today, when Islam spread north to Spain, the food came along. Today, the Sobrino de Bolin in Madrid is the oldest restaurant still in operation (1725).

With the wealth of culinary delights out there, it's a pity so many feel compelled to retreat to the comfort of a Starbucks, a KFC, or the Golden Arches. But in the case of McDonald's, some of its far-flung franchises have acquired rather exotic (albeit processed and chemically enhanced) dishes in addition to the old classics. For example, in New Zealand, there's the Kiwi Burger, a quarter-pound cheeseburger with beetroot and eggs. In Uruguay, there's the McHuevo, a hamburger with a poached egg and mayo. India has the Maharaja Mac, a lamb burger. Turkey has the Köfte Burger, a spiced patty inside a bun enriched with yogurt mix. The point is, if you absolutely must get your McFix while you're on the road (and these places are packed with travelers), you can at least give yourself a push to try something new.

With some foreign dishes, you may prefer to close your eyes. One restaurant in Switzerland beats you to it. The Blind Cow eatery in Zurich may have lights, but they choose not to use them. All diners enjoy their meal in complete darkness. No watches or phones are allowed to distract you from not being able to see your hand in front of your face. The waiters are blind and the diners are left to use their remaining four senses to navigate their way through the meal. There's a version in Beijing called Pitch Black, but the waiters there wear night-vision goggles.

Whether or not you can see your food, find it in a franchise familiar from back home, or find a waiter who can manage to get it to your table before you starve, the idea of dining abroad will, at the very least, continue to provide a rich source of material for stories for years to come.

BIGGEST-DRINKING TOURISTS

WINNER
British

AFRICA/MIDDLE EAST WINNER: South African
ASIA WINNER: Japanese
EUROPE WINNER: British
LATIN AMERICA WINNER: n/a
NORTH AMERICA WINNER: American
PACIFIC WINNER: Australia

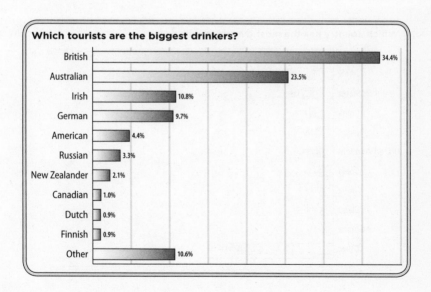

Which tourists are the biggest drinkers?

British	34.4%
Australian	23.5%
Irish	10.8%
German	9.7%
American	4.4%
Russian	3.3%
New Zealander	2.1%
Canadian	1.0%
Dutch	0.9%
Finnish	0.9%
Other	10.6%

TITANIC AWARD

COUNTRY WITH THE MOST OVERRATED CUISINE

WINNER

France

AFRICA/MIDDLE EAST WINNER: n/a
ASIA WINNER: China
EUROPE WINNER: France
LATIN AMERICA WINNER: Mexico
NORTH AMERICA WINNER: United States
PACIFIC WINNER: Australia

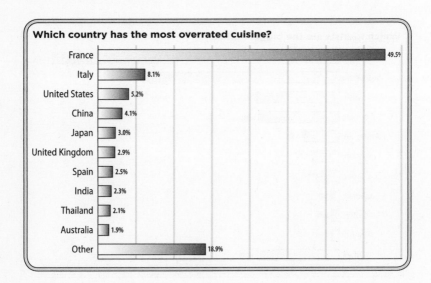

Which country has the most overrated cuisine?

Country	Percent
France	49.5%
Italy	8.1%
United States	5.2%
China	4.1%
Japan	3.0%
United Kingdom	2.9%
Spain	2.5%
India	2.3%
Thailand	2.1%
Australia	1.9%
Other	18.9%

COUNTRY WITH THE RUDEST WAITERS

WINNER

France

AFRICA/MIDDLE EAST WINNER: Israel/Turkey

ASIA WINNER: China

EUROPE WINNER: France

LATIN AMERICA WINNER: Argentina

NORTH AMERICA WINNER: United States

PACIFIC WINNER: Australia

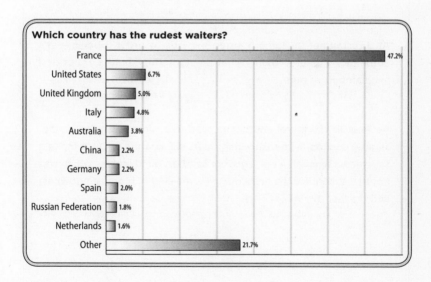

Which country has the rudest waiters?

Country	Percentage
France	47.2%
United States	6.7%
United Kingdom	5.0%
Italy	4.8%
Australia	3.8%
China	2.2%
Germany	2.2%
Spain	2.0%
Russian Federation	1.8%
Netherlands	1.6%
Other	21.7%

PERSONAL WORSTS
MEALS

When I was in Jordan, I was squatting beside Bedouins and eating rice with lamb chunks off this large communal plate. As the pile of food diminished, we realized we were eating right out of the head of a lamb. And then came the soup—a lamb's eye floating in broth. It turned in my mouth like a soft marble. Other bad meals were somewhat expected. I mean, if you order a hamburger in Dublin, you're asking for it.

—Keith Bellows, editor in chief of *National Geographic Traveler*

★

A patchy schnitzel of breaded cartilage in Sighisoara, Romania, back in 1999.   —Alex Robertson, travel writer, editor, and blogger

★

Pretty much every meal I ate in the Philippines. There's a good reason you don't see Filipino restaurants anywhere else.

—Tim Leffel, author of *The World's Cheapest Destinations*
and editor of *Perceptive Travel*

★

At a restaurant in Rome, I urged my kids to order a panini—"it's authentic," I assured them. What they got: three halves of hot dog in a hamburger bun.   —Norie Quintos, senior editor at
National Geographic Traveler

★

Hellhole at the literal end of the road in a Nicaraguan forest. Pig, slightly cooked, with razor-sharp hairs still coating it. Once made a seven-course meal out of a goat in Samburu-land, Kenya, which was not bad except for the first course (some kind of blood sundowner) and the last (brains).

—Jon Bowermaster, *National Geographic* writer, filmmaker, and kayaker

★

The octopus that ate Naples. In a tiny locals-only eatery, my wife and I ordered from the incomprehensible menu, trusting to chance. Chance delivered the biggest octopus in the history of Naples.

—Don George, creator of Don's Place, editor in chief of *Recce*, and contributing editor for *National Geographic Traveler*

★

The famous raw shrimp cocktail of Kathmandu. I ordered it to celebrate an overland trip into Tibet, got violent food poisoning, was sick for the next three weeks, and lost 16 pounds. Only then did it occur to me how far Kathmandu was from any ocean shrimp might live in.

—Catherine Watson, writer and former travel editor of the *Minneapolis Star Tribune*

★

The currywurst at the top of Berlin's Fernsehturm TV tower. It was my first foray into the wonderful culinary delights of currywurst, and it turned out to be nothing more than an outrageously overpriced Ball Park frank. Bonus: spending the better part of that night on the toilet praying for death!

—Mike Richard, editor of Vagabondish.com

★

Pisa, Italy. I got soggy fries and boiled chicken and two soft drinks. The total was $40. The cost plus the quality set a record for meal suckatude.

—Gary Arndt, travel blogger

TITANIC
SURVEY

TITANIC AWARD

COUNTRY WITH THE WORST BEER

WINNER
United States

AFRICA/MIDDLE EAST WINNER: Egypt
ASIA WINNER: China
EUROPE WINNER: United Kingdom
LATIN AMERICA WINNER: Jamaica/Mexico
NORTH AMERICA WINNER: United States
PACIFIC WINNER: Australia

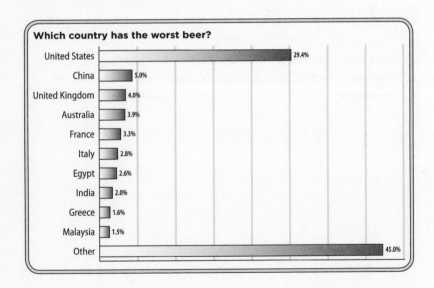

Which country has the worst beer?

Country	%
United States	29.4%
China	5.0%
United Kingdom	4.0%
Australia	3.9%
France	3.3%
Italy	2.8%
Egypt	2.6%
India	2.0%
Greece	1.6%
Malaysia	1.5%
Other	45.0%

COUNTRY WITH THE WORST NATIONAL CUISINE

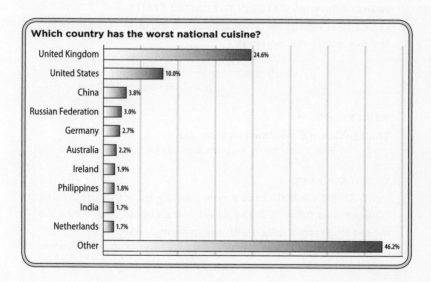

WINNER

United Kingdom

AFRICA/MIDDLE EAST WINNER: Egypt

ASIA WINNER: China

EUROPE WINNER: United Kingdom

LATIN AMERICA WINNER: Cuba

NORTH AMERICA WINNER: United States

PACIFIC WINNER: Australia

Which country has the worst national cuisine?

Country	%
United Kingdom	24.6%
United States	10.0%
China	3.8%
Russian Federation	3.0%
Germany	2.7%
Australia	2.2%
Ireland	1.9%
Philippines	1.8%
India	1.7%
Netherlands	1.7%
Other	46.2%

PERSONAL WORSTS
DRINKS

WORST BEER

It seems that anywhere outside the major metropolitan parts of the United States it's hazardous to drink anything but the American-made watered-down piss-liquid that's labeled "beer." And if you eschew it, you face potential harassment. In one such place, I ordered the only non-big-brewery beer on tap, and someone at the bar yelled out, "We've got ourselves a fancy beer drinker, boys." They were probably waiting for weeks for someone like me to come and order that. But I was saved by an empty keg (the bartender, in turn, quietly poured me a pint of the said piss-liquid, either because he assumed I'd drink it or because he was trying to save me from physical harm).

—David Farley, travel writer and author of *An Irreverent Curiosity*

WORST DRINKING WATER IN THE UNITED STATES

Los Angeles wins hands down. Do you like the taste of heavy metals and minerals in the morning?

—Peter Greenberg, investigative travel reporter and producer,
served as correspondent for ABC's *Good Morning America*
and travel editor for NBC's *Today* show

WORST WINE

Château Gue, a Zimbabwean Chenin Blanc.

—John Flinn, former executive travel editor, *San Francisco Chronicle*

WORST COCKTAIL

Lucky Cheng's in NYC. Total tourist trap (I went with tourists). The "Orgasm in a Bowl" is sticky sweet, Windex-blue, and tastes like melted Mr. Freezes spiked with cheap bathtub rum.

—Chantal Martineau, freelance travel, food, and drink writer,
and Travel Channel program host

WORST BAR TAB

WINNER

There may not be good records on the biggest bar tab—it's not the sort of thing people always report. But this one is certainly a contender: $216,608 for an unplanned evening on the town. A Middle Eastern businessman brought 17 friends with him to Crystal, a London club popular with the likes of Prince Harry. He started out with some relatively cheap wine ($50 a bottle), then moved on to $1,400 Dom Perignon magnums and a special eight-bottles-in-one of Cristal champagne for $60,000.

Fraser Donaldson, the club's spokesman, said the guest told the staff to keep the drinks flowing. By 5 a.m., the bill came to $216,608.

Source: *Edmonton Journal*, July 25, 2007

PERSONAL WORST

WORST QUESTION TO ASK AT A ROADSIDE FOOD STAND *Why is this meat so much cheaper than all the others?*

—Frank Bures, travel writer and contributing editor at WorldHum.com

PERSONAL WORSTS
DINING EXPERIENCES

WORST MENU ITEM IN AN ACTUAL RESTAURANT

Boiled Fermented Cow's Nose, Denpasar, Bali. (There is a note on this item, in English: "The flavor may not agree with some Western-ers." True, that.) —Tim Cahill, adventure travel writer, humorist, and author of many books, including *Lost in My Own Backyard*

WORST TRAIN STATION MENU

A restaurant in Greece offered "vagina" as one of the chef's speci-alities. I declined to try it.

—Martin Dunford, former publisher of the Rough Guides series

WORST FOOD

There is a tie for the most disgusting food I have tasted, between Turkish tripe soup (color, texture, and taste of wallpaper paste) and Sicilian vastedda (spleen burgers) that were basically the color and taste of feces. Both great local delicacies!

—Melissa Shales, guidebook writer, editor, and chairman of the British Guild of Travel Writers

WORST WAITS FOR DINNER

Caye Caulker, Belize. Restaurants on Caye Caulker are incredibly slow, even in light of the region's relaxed approach to time. On occasion, dinner arrives within an hour and a half.

—Alex Robertson Textor, travel writer, editor, and blogger

WORST STREET FOOD

Random pig organs reheated atop a sheet of corrugated metal. No idea which organs they were. Protein is hard to come by in some parts of the Andes.

—Thomas Kohnstamm, author of more than a dozen Lonely Planet guidebooks and *Do Travel Writers Go to Hell?*

WORST MILITARY FOOD

French MREs. You'd think they'd have this gourmet stuff, but they had two dozen flavors of greasy southern French crap that even the peasants wouldn't touch.

—Robert Young Pelton, filmmaker, speaker, and author of several books, including *The World's Most Dangerous Places*

TITANIC AWARD

COUNTRY WITH WORST-TASTING DRINKING WATER

WINNER
India

AFRICA/MIDDLE EAST WINNER: Egypt
ASIA WINNER: India
EUROPE WINNER: United Kingdom
LATIN AMERICA WINNER: Mexico
NORTH AMERICA WINNER: United States
PACIFIC WINNER: Australia

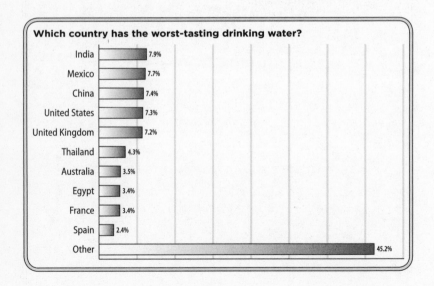

Which country has the worst-tasting drinking water?

Country	%
India	7.9%
Mexico	7.7%
China	7.4%
United States	7.3%
United Kingdom	7.2%
Thailand	4.3%
Australia	3.5%
Egypt	3.4%
France	3.4%
Spain	2.4%
Other	45.2%

TITANIC AWARD

WORST RESTAURANT NAMES

WINNER

Phat Phuc

1. Phat Phuc Noodle Bar (London, UK)

Credit: Joanna Siu

2. My Dung (Rosemead, California)

Credit: Heather Shelton

3. Stomach Clinic Railways Restaurant (Nairobi, Kenya)

Credit: Tom Harm

4. Vagina Tandori Indian Cuisine (Dublin, Ireland)

5. Cum-n-Eat (Fivemiletown, UK)

6. The Golden Shower Restaurant (Moshi, Tanzania)

7. Bung Hole (London, UK)

8. The Chocolate Log (Ganj, India)

9. Chewy Balls (Spring, Texas)

10. Soon Fatt Chinese Food (Bray, Ireland)

Sources: Signspotting.com, Oddee.com, BeltDriveBetty.com

PERSONAL WORST

WORST BEER *In a small village near Arusha, Tanzania, the local brew had chunky bits in it and was served in a bucket.*

—Carmen Roberts, reporter and producer for the BBC's *Fast Track*

PART 5

DESTINATIONS AND TOURISM

Travel is only glamorous in retrospect.

—PAUL THEROUX

Some years back I made a visit to Epcot Center. I realized that Walt Disney was a true visionary. Some people have said that the Epcot Pavilions do not reflect the countries they are supposed to represent. This might be true—for now. But they will soon. And it's not going to happen by redesigning or reforming Epcot; the world is what's going to change. As twisted as this may sound, the world is already changing to fit Disney's crafted version of it. The Epcot Center is, unlike Tomorrowland or Future World, a self-fulfilling prophecy.

Countries around the world are calling their historic treasures "attractions"; they make you buy a ticket and stand in line to see everything; nearly everyone speaks English (to help sell the postcards, T-shirts, and snow globes); and at least one person in every tour group I've ever seen, from the Great Pyramids to the Great Palace in Bangkok, is wearing something with Mickey Mouse on it. Some countries are even installing clean Western toilets for tourists.

As the world slowly turns on its axis and we evolve into one global

Epcot, cracks will no doubt appear where cultures go astray. It's happening already. Despite an overzealous tourism minister clinging to Walt Disney's playbook, some national characteristics are just too hard to shake off. But not all tourist destinations are that strategically scripted. Want proof? Read on.

TITANIC AWARD

LEAST RESPECTFUL PARKING

WINNER

Whether you're one of the thousands of visitors coming from around the world, or just from the center of London, it's never easy to find a parking spot during the Wimbledon tennis tournament in the outskirts of London. The neighborhood streets are typically clogged for weeks as players battle on the grass courts. In an effort to alleviate the parking problem (and pull in some extra revenue), nearby St. Mary's Church decided to sell parking spots for $33 a day. However, the church was also short on parking spots, so they let tennis fans park directly above gravesites in their cemetery. Reverend Mary Bide told the *Daily Mail* that "although the cars look 'odd,' they were only parked in the oldest part of the graveyard and funds raised would make a 'valuable contribution to the Church and the Diocese.'"   Source: *Daily Mail,* June 25, 2009

PERSONAL WORST

WORST PLACE IN THE ENTIRE WORLD   *Dubai is a gigantic expo of wrongness: everything that's bad about modern life brought together in one place. The only way to cross the street that goes right through the central business district is to take a taxi. I spent five days feeling like Charlton Heston at the end of* Planet of the Apes: *"We finally really did it! God damn you! God damn you all to hell!"*

—Tim Moore, British author of several travel books, including
I Believe in Yesterday and *Continental Drifter*

TITANIC AWARD

HARSHEST PUNISHMENT FOR LEWD DRUNKEN BEHAVIOR BY A TOURIST

WINNER

A liquored-up British tourist had his penis and testicles set ablaze by a local Greek woman. According to the police report, the Brit had pulled down his pants and exposed his one-eyed warrior to the females seated at the bar. He then "forcefully fondled" a 26-year-old local woman and asked her to grab hold of his trouser snake. When he refused to put away his pecker as she requested, she poured her Sabucco on it. When that failed to stop his advances, she ignited his alcohol-soaked jewels with a lighter.

The Briton was taken to a private clinic for second-degree genitalia burns. The Greek woman turned herself over to the police following the event. The case was presented in court, and the woman, who had become something of a national hero, was freed by the magistrate and prosecutor for acting in self-defense. Which Greek god do you suppose would get jurisdiction over this incident? Source: *Daily Telegraph*, August 6, 2009

PERSONAL WORST

WORST BEACH *Condado Beach, San Juan, Puerto Rico. While I was there, a 13-year-old boy drowned. As the rescue team searched for his body well into the next day, another man swimming there also drowned, right next to the searchers.*

—Johnny Jet (aka John E. DiScala), founder/editor of JohnnyJet.com

---

TITANIC AWARD

TITANIC
SURVEY

CHEAPEST TOURISTS

WINNER

British

AFRICA/MIDDLE EAST WINNER: Israeli
ASIA WINNER: Chinese
EUROPE WINNER: British
LATIN AMERICA WINNER: Mexican
NORTH AMERICA WINNER: American
PACIFIC WINNER: Australian

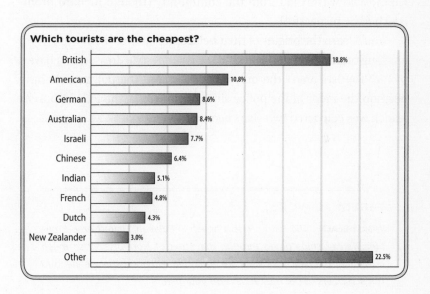

Which tourists are the cheapest?

British	18.8%
American	10.8%
German	8.6%
Australian	8.4%
Israeli	7.7%
Chinese	6.4%
Indian	5.1%
French	4.8%
Dutch	4.3%
New Zealander	3.0%
Other	22.5%

TITANIC AWARD

LEAST WELCOME TOUR

WINNER

Want to know what it's like to have a polygamous relationship? For $69.95 Richard and Heber Holm will show you. No, not that way. They'll sell you a ticket to board "The Polygamy Experience" bus tour. On this four-hour guided offering, they will explain the story of "the U.S.'s largest and most secluded polygamist colony." What better way to blend in and mingle with the notoriously withdrawn fundamentalist Mormons than on a 29-passenger bus with a tour leader (Richard Holm) who was exiled from the community (though Richard promised he'd be respectful).

You'll learn the origins of their beliefs, get answers about the women's long braids and *Little House on the Prairie*–style dresses, and have a picnic. Tourists aren't the only ones watching. The polygamists have been on the radar of the police since Warren Jeffs, the FLDS Church's leader, was convicted two years ago. Source: News.com.au, September 21, 2009

PERSONAL WORST

WORST BEACH *The Hilton Resort beach in Fujairah, United Arab Emirates. Tanker ships going through the Strait of Hormuz spill so much crude that the beach showers are equipped with industrial cleaner and pot scrubbers to get the tar balls off your feet.*

—Spud Hilton, travel editor for the San Francisco Chronicle

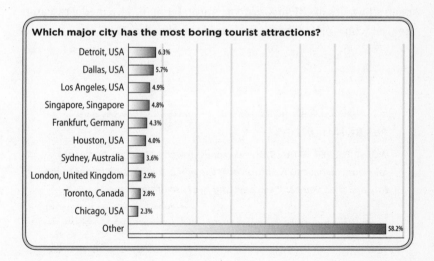

TITANIC AWARD

CITY WITH MOST BORING TOURIST ATTRACTIONS (OF TOP 100 CITIES)

WINNER

Detroit, Michigan, USA

AFRICA/MIDDLE EAST WINNER: Ankara, Turkey

ASIA WINNER: Singapore

EUROPE WINNER: Frankfurt, Germany

LATIN AMERICA WINNER: Lima, Peru

NORTH AMERICA WINNER: Detroit, Michigan, USA

PACIFIC WINNER: Sydney, Australia

Which major city has the most boring tourist attractions?

City	%
Detroit, USA	6.3%
Dallas, USA	5.7%
Los Angeles, USA	4.9%
Singapore, Singapore	4.8%
Frankfurt, Germany	4.3%
Houston, USA	4.0%
Sydney, Australia	3.6%
London, United Kingdom	2.9%
Toronto, Canada	2.8%
Chicago, USA	2.3%
Other	58.2%

TITANIC AWARD

MOST AWKWARD PARK TO BRING YOUR KIDS TO

WINNER

The High Line

What do you get when you cross a new boutique hotel and a new urban walkway? A free sex show. New York's Standard hotel and the High Line walkway have intersected to create this unusual by-product.

With scores of New Yorkers and tourists walking under and beside the hotel's floor-to-ceiling windows, randy hotel guests have taken the opportunity to show off their reproduction skills. Or simply practice a bit of exhibitionism.

There are now people flocking to the new park only to see a free peep show. "It's like *Wild Kingdom*," Aaron Lipman, 34, a media research analyst who works near the park, told the *New York Post*.

Source: *New York Post*, September 2, 2009

PERSONAL WORST

WORST TOURIST ATTRACTION *Petronas Towers, Malaysia. Sure, they're tall—but you have to wait forever in line and pay admission to get to the top, and then you can't see anything because of the haze.*

—Vivek Wagle, Lonely Planet's website editor

TITANIC AWARD

MOST CROWDED BEACH

WINNER
Saraswati, India

The camera lens isn't quite wide enough to capture all 22 million bathers gathered on the banks of the mythical Saraswati River in Allahabad, India. They came to take a holy dip during the "most auspicious day" of Maha Kumbh Mela (Great Pitcher Fair). Roughly 70 million took part in the six-week festival—the world's largest religious gathering.

Credit: AP/John McConnico

TITANIC AWARD

MOST CROWDED POOL

WINNER

Tokyo's Korakuen Pool

Here's the scary part—Tokyo's Korakuen Pool gets even more crowded. There are about 16,000 people pictured here. At its peak, the population reaches 30,000 swimmers. At that point, you can't even see the water—it looks more like a rock concert. Or a giant Japanese subway car.

Credit: AP/Kasahara

CITY WITH THE UGLIEST ARCHITECTURE (OF TOP 100 CITIES)

WINNER
Los Angeles, California, USA

AFRICA/MIDDLE EAST WINNER: Ankara, Turkey

ASIA WINNER: Beijing, China

EUROPE WINNER: Moscow, Russia

LATIN AMERICA WINNER: São Paulo, Brazil

NORTH AMERICA WINNER: Los Angeles, California, USA

PACIFIC WINNER: Sydney, Australia

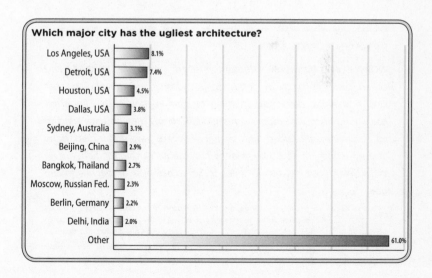

Which major city has the ugliest architecture?

City	Percentage
Los Angeles, USA	8.1%
Detroit, USA	7.4%
Houston, USA	4.5%
Dallas, USA	3.8%
Sydney, Australia	3.1%
Beijing, China	2.9%
Bangkok, Thailand	2.7%
Moscow, Russian Fed.	2.3%
Berlin, Germany	2.2%
Delhi, India	2.0%
Other	61.0%

TITANIC AWARD

MOST SPECIALIZED TOUR GUIDE

WINNER
Wuhan

Visitors to the Chinese city of Wuhan, in Hubei province, are in good hands when nature calls. Specialized "toilet guides" with easy-to-spot red armbands have been hired by the city to patrol tourist spots and assist visitors in need of restrooms. The fee for this special service is 3.8 cents.

Source: Changjiang Commercial News, March 24, 2007

PERSONAL WORST

WORST ISLAND TO INHABIT *Clipperton Island. Surrounded by sharks and covered with eerily squawking boobies and beady-eyed red crabs that swarm at night, devouring anything organic in their path, Clipperton has a long history of repelling human life. Nearly all who have tried to inhabit this Pacific Island (and many have tried) have either died, gone insane, or both. The U.S. Navy planned to establish an airstrip here during World War II but lost several ships trying to establish a beachhead and gave up.*

—Charles Veley, quite possibly the world's most traveled person, having been to 709 of the world's 757 various countries, territories, autonomous regions, enclaves, geographically separated island groups, major states, and provinces

TITANIC AWARD

CITY THAT FEELS MOST DANGEROUS (OF TOP 100 CITIES)

WINNER
Johannesburg, South Africa

AFRICA/MIDDLE EAST WINNER: Johannesburg, South Africa
ASIA WINNER: Karachi, Pakistan
EUROPE WINNER: London, UK
LATIN AMERICA WINNER: Rio de Janeiro, Brazil
NORTH AMERICA WINNER: Detroit, Michigan, USA
PACIFIC WINNER: n/a

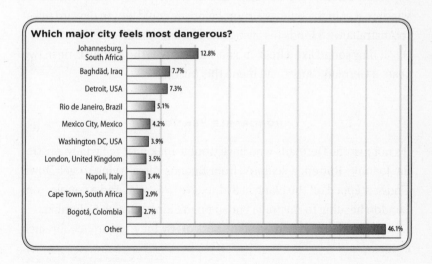

Which major city feels most dangerous?

Johannesburg, South Africa	12.8%
Baghdād, Iraq	7.7%
Detroit, USA	7.3%
Rio de Janeiro, Brazil	5.1%
Mexico City, Mexico	4.2%
Washington DC, USA	3.9%
London, United Kingdom	3.5%
Napoli, Italy	3.4%
Cape Town, South Africa	2.9%
Bogotá, Colombia	2.7%
Other	46.1%

TITANIC AWARD

MOST MISGUIDED TRAVELER

WINNER

If Australia's tourist campaign doesn't seem to be hitting its visitor quota, it's not necessarily a case of failed marketing. It could also be failed geography. Or spelling. A 21-year-old German traveler booked a ticket to Sydney to visit his girlfriend. At least he thought he did. If he had looked a bit closer, he would have seen that it was a ticket to Sidney, Montana, which is exactly where he ended up after misspelling the destination when booking his ticket online.

You'd think the sight of Canada out the window might have given it away. He was certainly caught off guard by the winter weather. He was expecting summer in Australia, but was stuck for three days with a thin windbreaker in the Billings airport before he could buy an onward ticket to Australia with funds his friends and family wired.

It may sound like a freak mixup, but this was the second time in two years a German tourist had made this mistake.

HONORABLE MENTIONS

It's not just the Germans who have trouble making it to Sydney, Australia. Joannes Rutten, a sculptor from Buenos Aires trying to get Down Under, stepped off the plane in Sydney, Nova Scotia. And a couple from London heading to Australia ended up in Sidney, British Columbia.

Maybe there should be some sort of "Sydney" insurance for such events.

Source: *San Francisco Chronicle*, December 28, 2008; Reuters, December 29, 2006; *New Republic*, August 18, 2009

TITANIC AWARD

CITY WITH LAMEST NIGHTLIFE (OF TOP 100 CITIES)

WINNER

Baghdad, Iraq

AFRICA/MIDDLE EAST WINNER: Baghdad, Iraq
ASIA WINNER: Beijing, China
EUROPE WINNER: Frankfurt, Germany
NORTH AMERICA WINNER: Detroit, Michigan, USA
PACIFIC WINNER: Sydney, Australia

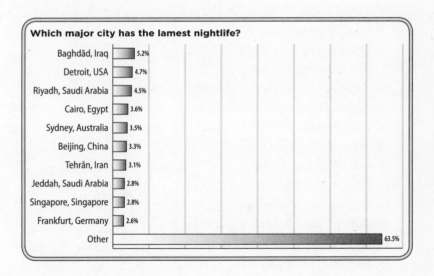

Which major city has the lamest nightlife?

City	Percentage
Baghdăd, Iraq	5.2%
Detroit, USA	4.7%
Riyadh, Saudi Arabia	4.5%
Cairo, Egypt	3.6%
Sydney, Australia	3.5%
Beijing, China	3.3%
Tehrăn, Iran	3.1%
Jeddah, Saudi Arabia	2.8%
Singapore, Singapore	2.8%
Frankfurt, Germany	2.6%
Other	63.5%

TITANIC AWARD

MOST UNFORTUNATE CITY NAMES

WINNER

Dildo

1. Dildo, Newfoundland, Canada
2. Fucking, Austria
3. Beaver Lick, Kentucky, USA
4. Shitterton, UK
5. Tightwad, Missouri, USA
6. Swastika, Ontario, Canada
7. Mianus, Connecticut, USA
8. Spread Eagle, Newfoundland, Canada
9. Puke, Albania
10. Twatt, Shetland Islands, Scotland
11. Windpassing, Austria
12. Big Bone Lick State Park, Kentucky, USA
13. Stalker, Pennsylvania, USA
14. Why, Arizona, USA
15. Crapo, Maryland, USA
16. Hell, Michigan, USA
17. Climax, Michigan, USA
18. Intercourse, Pennsylvania, USA
19. Stoner, British Columbia, Canada
20. Blue Ball, Pennsylvania, USA
21. Sexmoan, Philippines
22. Big Knob, Kentucky, USA
23. Lost, Scotland
24. Hygiene, Colorado, USA

25. Wetwang, UK
26. Ass, Ukraine
27. Boring, Oregon, USA
28. Mysore, India
29. Condom, France
30. Unalaska, Alaska, USA

PERSONAL WORSTS
ATTRACTIONS

Empire State Building. We waited for two hours, then there wasn't much to see once we arrived at the top. Would have rather spent my time and money at the top of 30 Rockefeller Plaza.
—Sture Bjarnelind, travel editor for *Aftonbladet*, Sweden's largest newspaper

★

Pisa. There's a building there. It leans. End of conversation.
—Peter Greenberg, investigative travel reporter and producer, served as correspondent for ABC's *Good Morning America* and travel editor for NBC's *Today* show

★

This has to be the London Eye. Incredibly expensive, and not even a building but a fairground attraction. Other cities have more class. And better views.
—Martin Dunford, former publisher of the Rough Guides series

★

The Bunyip in Murray Bridge, South Australia. Insert a coin and a crappy plastic creature emerges from a pond strewn with rubbish. Brilliant!
—Peter Moore, Australian travel writer and author of several books, including *Vroom with a View*

MOST UNNECESSARILY CHALLENGING MEANS OF TRANSPORTATION

WINNERS

Markus Eriksen and Joel Paschal

As if crossing the Pacific isn't hard enough, professional adventurers Dr. Markus Eriksen and marine scientist Joel Paschal made the 2,600-mile journey on a raft made of plastic bottles and other trash. The pair left Long Beach, California, on June 1 on a 30-foot vessel constructed from sailboat masts, six pontoons filled with 15 plastic bottles, and a cabin made from the fuselage of a Cessna airplane—and arrived three months later.

HONORABLE MENTIONS

- Neil Sauter, 24, completed an 830-mile trek on stilts across Michigan in eight weeks, averaging 15 miles per day.

- Tony Hawks, in order to win a bet, hitchhiked around the circumference of Ireland while carrying a refrigerator—the half-size version. Still, it's a little too heavy to tuck under your arm and walk down the street. Though it would presumably save on minibar expenses.

- Thor Heyerdahl, the grand master of making trips difficult, took a pae-pae raft make of balsa wood (the *Kon-Tiki*) and sailed it 4,300 miles, from South America to the Tuamotu Islands.

Source: Associated Press, August 28, 2008; *Traverse City Record-Eagle*,
June 2, 2008; Tony Hawks's book *Round Ireland with a Fridge*

TITANIC AWARD

MOST IRONIC TOURIST ATTRACTION FOR NONDRINKERS

WINNER

Buddhist Monks

In Khun Han, Thailand, near the Cambodian border, Buddhist monks are hard at work adding to their 20-structure compound. The building materials may be a slight departure from Buddhist tradition. They're using empty beer bottles. Since 1984, they've already used 1.5 million bottles. One structure, known as Wat Pa Maha Chedi Kaew, is also known as Wat Lan Kuad (the Temple of a Million Bottles). It's a mix of green Heineken bottles and the local brown bottles from Chang beer. The bottles let in light, are easy to clean, and if you overlook the fact that Buddhist monks aren't supposed to drink alcohol or encourage its consumption, it's not a bad plan. Even the mosaics of Buddha are created with bottle caps. That's one way to attract a new generation of followers.

Source: *Daily Telegraph*, February 18, 2009

PERSONAL WORST

WORST TOURIST INFORMATION OFFICE *Plovdiv, Bulgaria. The booth was open two hours a day and they didn't speak English. I don't think they spoke Bulgarian.*

—Patrick Smith, commercial airline pilot, air travel columnist for *Salon*, and author

---

CITY WITH THE WORST SHOPPING (OF TOP 100 CITIES)

WINNER

Baghdad, Iraq

AFRICA/MIDDLE EAST WINNER: Baghdad, Iraq
ASIA WINNER: Yangon, Myanmar
EUROPE WINNER: Moscow, Russia
NORTH AMERICA WINNER: Detroit, Michigan, USA
PACIFIC WINNER: Sydney, Australia

Which major city has the worst shopping?

City	%
Baghdäd, Iraq	6.8%
Adis Abeba, Ethiopia	4.7%
Detroit, USA	4.7%
Cairo, Egypt	3.8%
Yangon, Myanmar (Burma)	3.4%
Dhaka, Bangladesh	3.2%
Tehrän, Iran	2.9%
Houston, USA	2.7%
Sydney, Australia	2.7%
Moscow, Russian Fed.	2.5%
Other	64.0%

COUNTRY WITH THE DIRTIEST BEACHES

WINNER

India

AFRICA/MIDDLE EAST WINNER: Egypt
ASIA WINNER: Malaysia
EUROPE WINNER: United Kingdom
LATIN AMERICA WINNER: Mexico
NORTH AMERICA WINNER: United States
PACIFIC WINNER: Indonesia

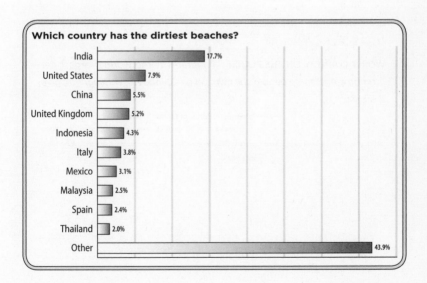

Which country has the dirtiest beaches?

Country	Percentage
India	17.7%
United States	7.9%
China	5.5%
United Kingdom	5.2%
Indonesia	4.3%
Italy	3.8%
Mexico	3.1%
Malaysia	2.5%
Spain	2.4%
Thailand	2.0%
Other	43.9%

TITANIC AWARD

WORST FESTIVAL SOUVENIR

WINNER

Byryeong City Mud Festival

Tourists joined thousands of Koreans in celebrating the Byryeong City Mud Festival. Events included mud-wrestling, mud-sliding, mud-prison, mud-bathing, and mud-everything-else. Much to the dismay of the muddy participants, a bacteria in the mud left hundreds hospitalized with dermatological maladies. Source: *Daily Mail*, July 12, 2009

PERSONAL WORST

WORST COUNTRY ON THE PLANET *Mauritania is the world's largest cat litter box. And some people still own slaves. Chinguetti, shminguetti; give it a miss.*

—Jeff Greenwald, director of Ethical Traveler, travel writer, performer, and author of several books, including *Size of the World*

COUNTRY WITH THE MOST HARASSING TOUTS/STREET VENDORS

WINNER

Egypt

AFRICA/MIDDLE EAST WINNER: Egypt
ASIA WINNER: India
EUROPE WINNER: Italy
LATIN AMERICA WINNER: Mexico
NORTH AMERICA WINNER: United States
PACIFIC WINNER: Australia

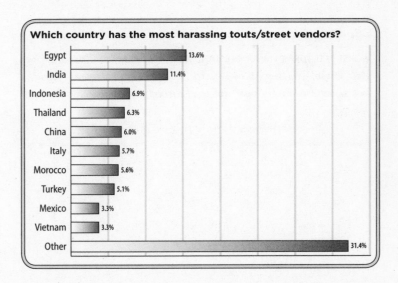

Which country has the most harassing touts/street vendors?

Country	Percentage
Egypt	13.6%
India	11.4%
Indonesia	6.9%
Thailand	6.3%
China	6.0%
Italy	5.7%
Morocco	5.6%
Turkey	5.1%
Mexico	3.3%
Vietnam	3.3%
Other	31.4%

EDITOR'S CHOICE

TITANIC AWARD

WORST MUSEUM SECURITY

WINNER

Ohashi Collection Kan Museum

You might even say they were asking for it. The Ohashi Collection Kan Museum in Takayama kept their prized 220-pound gold bullion unguarded, unprotected by sensors, and out in the open, without so much as a glass case to keep people from grabbing it. Curators wanted visitors to be able to touch it. Three masked men touched it, all right. In broad daylight, they made off with the $2.1 million gold bar. The biggest surprise was that local police officer Shinji Kurake was "shocked" by the heist.

Source: Associated Press, March 19, 2007

PERSONAL WORST

WORST CULTURAL MISUNDERSTANDING *Mispronounce "papaya" in Vietnamese—you've said the F word. At Hanoi's central market a quick exit saved me from a near riot that ensued after I "insulted" a fruit vendor.*

—Dave Lowe, travel writer and author of *Sandwiches Should NEVER Taste Like Cow Crap*

TITANIC AWARD

COUNTRY WITH THE MOST AGGRESSIVE BEGGARS

WINNER

India

AFRICA/MIDDLE EAST WINNER: Egypt
ASIA WINNER: India
EUROPE WINNER: Italy
LATIN AMERICA WINNER: Mexico
NORTH AMERICA WINNER: United States
PACIFIC WINNER: Australia

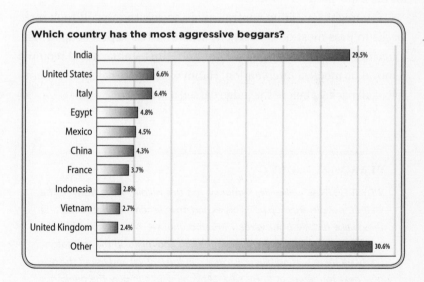

Which country has the most aggressive beggars?

Country	Percentage
India	29.5%
United States	6.6%
Italy	6.4%
Egypt	4.8%
Mexico	4.5%
China	4.3%
France	3.7%
Indonesia	2.8%
Vietnam	2.7%
United Kingdom	2.4%
Other	30.6%

TITANIC AWARD

WORST WAY TO CARRY DRUGS THROUGH CUSTOMS

WINNER

Things could have gone even worse for a 48-year-old named Hatim. He was arrested at Toronto International Airport in April for transporting cocaine into the country. He had swallowed an impressive 76 packets of it to get the stash through customs on his way back from Buenos Aires, and then had to keep his bowels under control. That's a total weight of one kilogram of cocaine (a value of $100,000) that would have cost him his life if any packet ruptured.

You might say Hatim controlled his bowels too well. It took three weeks to pass most of the packets, as authorities kept a bedpan vigil. Three of the packets became lodged in Hatim's stomach and required removal by medical intervention. Hatim was able to safely divest himself of all packets before the judge passed a sentence.   Source: UPI, April 29, 2009

PERSONAL WORST

WORST FESTIVAL   *Pikeville, Kentucky, has this Hillbilly Days festival. The well-off people dress up as hillbillies and drive around in floats depicting things like hillbilly front yards with an outhouse. Who's watching? The actual hillbillies. They come in from the hills and make up the spectators. I noticed there was no bluegrass music in the festival and asked the hillbilly next to me about it. He said: "Anyone who can play the banjo got the f*ck out of here."*

—Joe Sharkey, travel columnist for the *New York Times*

TITANIC AWARD

COUNTRY WITH THE WORST SOUVENIRS

WINNER

United States

AFRICA/MIDDLE EAST WINNER: Egypt

ASIA WINNER: China

EUROPE WINNER: United Kingdom

LATIN AMERICA WINNER: Mexico

NORTH AMERICA WINNER: United States

PACIFIC WINNER: Australia

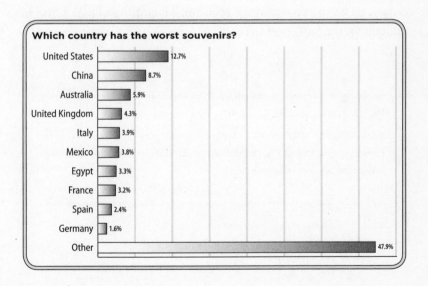

Which country has the worst souvenirs?

United States	12.7%
China	8.7%
Australia	5.9%
United Kingdom	4.3%
Italy	3.9%
Mexico	3.8%
Egypt	3.3%
France	3.2%
Spain	2.4%
Germany	1.6%
Other	47.9%

TITANIC AWARD

WORST PLANTED DRUGS

WINNER

Japanese Customs

A passenger who passed through Japan's Narita International Airport found a little surprise in his luggage when he got home: five ounces of cannabis, courtesy of the customs staff.

Apparently a customs officer hid the package in a randomly selected suitcase as a way to test the airport security staff. But then the drug-sniffing dogs couldn't manage to find the marijuana, and the officer couldn't recall which bag he put it in.

There was no note with the gift (and no rolling paper either).

Because Japan has such strict laws for narcotics, including jail sentences for the possession of even small quantities of pot, it may be difficult for the passenger to return it. Source: BBC, May 26, 2008

PERSONAL WORST

WORST TOURIST INFORMATION *Office: "Good afternoon, sir, and welcome to Hoi An [Vietnam]. I have information for hotels, beach location, and prostitute sex. And also car hire."*

—Benji Lanyado, travel writer for the *Guardian*

COUNTRY WHOSE LOCALS GIVE THE WORST DIRECTIONS TO TRAVELERS

WINNER

France

AFRICA/MIDDLE EAST WINNER: Egypt

ASIA WINNER: China

EUROPE WINNER: France

LATIN AMERICA WINNER: Mexico

NORTH AMERICA WINNER: United States

PACIFIC WINNER: Australia

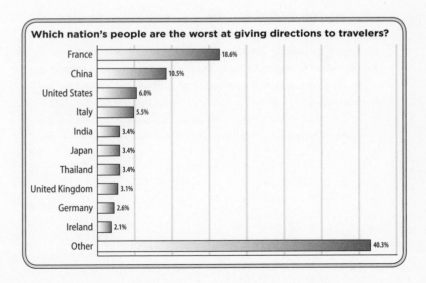

Which nation's people are the worst at giving directions to travelers?

Country	Percentage
France	18.6%
China	10.5%
United States	6.0%
Italy	5.5%
India	3.4%
Japan	3.4%
Thailand	3.4%
United Kingdom	3.1%
Germany	2.6%
Ireland	2.1%
Other	40.3%

TITANIC AWARD

WORST SEARCH AND RESCUE

WINNER
Chinese S&R Crew

While looking for a missing tourist on China's Taishan Mountain (one of the country's Five Sacred Peaks), rescuers came up empty. However, they did manage to find the corpses of seven other people they were previously unable to find. Not sure if their "better late than never" approach works so well with search and rescue.   Source: Reuters, May 5, 2009

PERSONAL WORST

WORST OVERRUN SACRED SPOT *The tiny cemetery on the island of Janitzio in Lake Patzcuaro during Mexico's Day of the Dead. Tourism officials were promoting the place to death—no pun intended—and it seemed that all of Mexico had descended upon the cemetery, trampling graves, pushing one another, ruining what is otherwise a beautiful, sacred tradition.*

—Jim Benning, founder and editor of WorldHum.com

LAMEST MAJOR CASINO IN LAS VEGAS

WINNER

Circus Circus

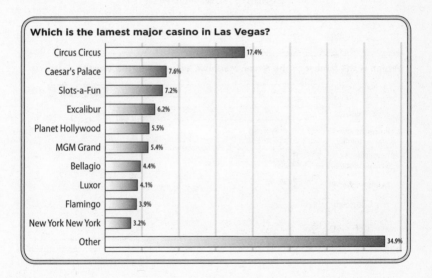

Which is the lamest major casino in Las Vegas?

Casino	Percentage
Circus Circus	17.4%
Caesar's Palace	7.6%
Slots-a-Fun	7.2%
Excalibur	6.2%
Planet Hollywood	5.5%
MGM Grand	5.4%
Bellagio	4.4%
Luxor	4.1%
Flamingo	3.9%
New York New York	3.2%
Other	34.9%

PERSONAL WORST

WORST ISLAND *Easter Island. I thought it was pretty miserable—expensive, uninteresting food, my hotel was a dump, and it was hard to engage with the local community, unlike the rest of Chile, where it's easy to strike up conversation. The statues were cool, but the island just didn't have a warm and welcoming feel. I wasn't sad to get on the flight back.*

—Paul Brady, freelance writer and former editor of Jaunted.com

TITANIC AWARD

LAMEST MEDIEVAL WONDER OF THE WORLD

WINNER

Leaning Tower of Pisa

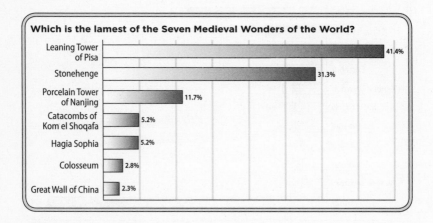

Which is the lamest of the Seven Medieval Wonders of the World?

Wonder	Percentage
Leaning Tower of Pisa	41.4%
Stonehenge	31.3%
Porcelain Tower of Nanjing	11.7%
Catacombs of Kom el Shoqafa	5.2%
Hagia Sophia	5.2%
Colosseum	2.8%
Great Wall of China	2.3%

PERSONAL WORST

WORST FLIES *Australia's Northern Territory. They'll literally drink the water off your eyeballs.*

—Jason Cochran, travel writer, guidebook author, and blogger

TITANIC AWARD

WORST SOUVENIR SMUGGLING

WINNER

When a 29-year-old Washington State native named Gypsy returned from a trip to Thailand, she decided to bring a rhesus monkey with her. As it turns out, this is illegal. At least it is the way she did it, which was sedating the monkey, stashing it under her blouse, and posing as a pregnant woman.

She succeeded in getting the monkey by customs in Thailand, the gate agents, the flight crew, and even U.S. Customs in Los Angeles.

It was only later, when Gypsy boasted of her clever smuggling stunt to a clothing-store clerk, that she got busted. Her mother had accompanied her on the flight from Thailand, and she got busted, too. A jury found them both guilty.   Source: *Daily Mail*, December 9, 2008

HONORABLE MENTION

A 56-year-old woman from the Czech Republic traveling from Samoa was arrested for trying to smuggle three banana plants into Australia in her underwear. How this woman could walk or sit on a plane with three banana plants in her underwear may be more of a mystery than why she was transporting them. One more surprise: the maximum penalty for this is 10 years in jail and a $66,000 fine.

Source: *Sydney Morning Herald*, October 24, 2008

TITANIC AWARD

LAMEST "MODERN" WONDER OF THE WORLD

WINNER

CN Tower

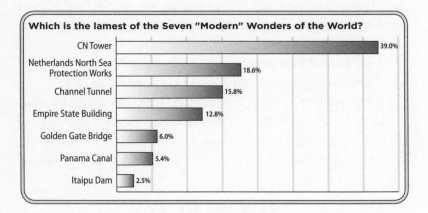

Which is the lamest of the Seven "Modern" Wonders of the World?

CN Tower	39.0%
Netherlands North Sea Protection Works	18.6%
Channel Tunnel	15.8%
Empire State Building	12.8%
Golden Gate Bridge	6.0%
Panama Canal	5.4%
Itaipu Dam	2.5%

PERSONAL WORST

WORST TRAVEL ILLNESS   *La Paz, Bolivia. I had just finished biking across the Amazon from Brazil in 40 days. I noticed I had a high fever after dinner. I could barely walk back to the hotel. I spent four days with a temp over 40 degrees Celsius (104 Fahrenheit). I took Japanese medicine for fever and my temp shot down to 34.8 Celsius (94.6 F)—and it felt like I was flying. That concerned me. So I took the next flight back to Tokyo—it took me 72 hours on four flights to get home. I checked into the hospital when I landed and stayed there for 21 days. Turns out I had typhoid fever.*

—Nori Kunori, Japanese adventurer, travel writer, and professor

WORST REASON TO SUE YOUR TRAVEL AGENT

WINNER

When a 60-year-old tourist named Zhou was pushed off a 20-foot-high rock face by a monkey in China's Chengdu Wildlife Park, she wanted someone to sue for her suffering (fractured hip and broken ribs). Since the monkey (who got upset when she didn't hand over the monkey food she bought) wasn't exactly able to pay, she turned around and sued her . . . travel agent. Yep, it was apparently the travel agent's fault. If you can't sue the one you want, sue the one who booked your trip.

Source: *Metro UK*, September 18, 2009

PERSONAL WORST

WORST TOURIST ATTRACTION   *About an hour outside Guangzhou, China, somebody has built a sort of rural-living theme park, complete with cockfights, pigs being dropped into water from great heights, and throbbing music by that great Chinese folk artist Cher. Ideal on a 100-degree summer day.*

—Christopher Reynolds, travel writer for the *Los Angeles Times*

TITANIC AWARD

LAMEST NATURAL WONDER OF THE WORLD

WINNER

Harbor of Rio de Janeiro

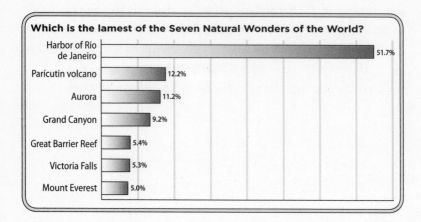

Which is the lamest of the Seven Natural Wonders of the World?

Harbor of Rio de Janeiro	51.7%
Parícutin volcano	12.2%
Aurora	11.2%
Grand Canyon	9.2%
Great Barrier Reef	5.4%
Victoria Falls	5.3%
Mount Everest	5.0%

PERSONAL WORST

WORST CAMPING SPOT *Tied into a guardrail beside a road in the black of night in New Paltz, New York. I couldn't see at all, no light, and was terrified I was going to fall off.*

—Will Gadd, elite adventure athlete

WORST RULES FOR SPRING BREAK

WINNER
Daytona Beach

Sounds like Daytona Beach, Florida, is trying to find an extra revenue stream for the police—or throw a wrench into the spring break activities. Included in the local rules aimed at the hordes of frolicking, inebriated tourists are:

- No drunken swimming
- No use of drugs while under the influence of alcohol (though it seems drug use would be enough to make an arrest)
- No molesting trash cans
- No sex unless using the missionary position

Source: Jaunted.com, September 2, 2009

PERSONAL WORST

WORST NAME FOR A NIGHTCLUB *The Disco of the Giant Ground Sloth, Puerto Natales, Chile.*

—Tim Cahill, adventure travel writer, humorist, and author of many books,
including *Lost in My Own Backyard*

TITANIC AWARD

LAMEST "NEW" WONDER OF THE WORLD

WINNER

Christ the Redeemer

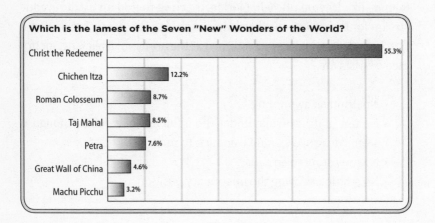

Which is the lamest of the Seven "New" Wonders of the World?

Christ the Redeemer	55.3%
Chichen Itza	12.2%
Roman Colosseum	8.7%
Taj Mahal	8.5%
Petra	7.6%
Great Wall of China	4.6%
Machu Picchu	3.2%

PERSONAL WORST

WORST TRAVEL BOOK   *Alain de Botton's* Art of Travel—*I can't remember anything about it.*

—Ginny Light, assistant travel editor for the *Times* Online

WORST SURVIVAL-SAFETY REGULATION

EDITOR'S CHOICE

WINNER
BBC

Sir Robin Knox-Johnston may have been the first person to sail single-handedly and nonstop around the world, but that doesn't make him exempt from following safety procedures. At least not according to BBC producers, who took out a "telephone-book-size" set of regulations during the filming of an adventure documentary and ordered him not to light a portable stove unless a "safety advisor" was supervising it.

Source: *Daily Mail*, April 18, 2009

PERSONAL WORST

WORST HAIRCUT WHILE TRAVELING *I should have known better, but when I was living in Prague, I went to a tacky salon on the outskirts of town—they're usually called Salon Barbara or something like that—just for a quick cut. In my faltering Czech I said that I wanted a little off the top and sides and more off the back. Instead, she did the opposite, and I ended up with a mullet.*

—David Farley, travel writer and author of *An Irreverent Curiosity*

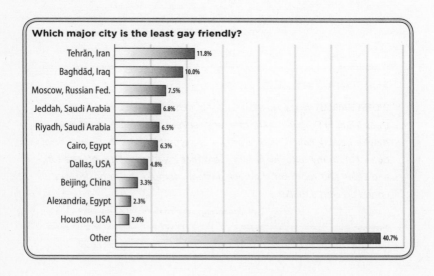

LEAST GAY-FRIENDLY MAJOR CITY

WINNER

Tehran, Iran

AFRICA/MIDDLE EAST WINNER: Tehran, Iran

ASIA WINNER: Beijing, China

EUROPE WINNER: Moscow, Russia

LATIN AMERICA WINNER: Bogotá, Colombia

NORTH AMERICA WINNER: Dallas, Texas, USA

PACIFIC WINNER: Sydney, Australia

Which major city is the least gay friendly?

City	%
Tehrăn, Iran	11.8%
Baghdăd, Iraq	10.0%
Moscow, Russian Fed.	7.5%
Jeddah, Saudi Arabia	6.8%
Riyadh, Saudi Arabia	6.5%
Cairo, Egypt	6.3%
Dallas, USA	4.8%
Beijing, China	3.3%
Alexandria, Egypt	2.3%
Houston, USA	2.0%
Other	40.7%

TITANIC AWARD

WORST TOUR THEME

WINNER

If you're trying to breathe a little life into your city's tourism industry, there seems to be one basic rule: anything goes. Thus Warsaw's Szarpie Travel Agency has begun taking tourists to the CIA's alleged detention center in the northern Mazuria region of Poland (or as close as they're allowed to get). Visitors will be able to "cycle and canoe near the Polish intelligence service's training centre," Joanna Sobieska told the PAP news agency. The Polish training facilities at Stare Kiejkuty and Szymany have been in the news as interrogation centers for terror suspects. Washington has acknowledged that it has held suspects in secret outside U.S. territory, and several countries have facilitated covert U.S. flights, but since both the United States and Poland deny this facility exists, tourism to the area shouldn't be a problem.

Source: Agence France-Presse, February 22, 2007

PERSONAL WORST

WORST RIP-OFF *This award is shared by the various five-star international hotels that insist on charging exorbitant fees for Internet access. At the Athens Hilton, Wi-Fi is $30 a day! (And a Coke from the minibar is $8.50.)*

—Patrick Smith, commercial airline pilot, air travel columnist for *Salon*, and author

MOST EASILY FOOLED TOURISTS

WINNER

American

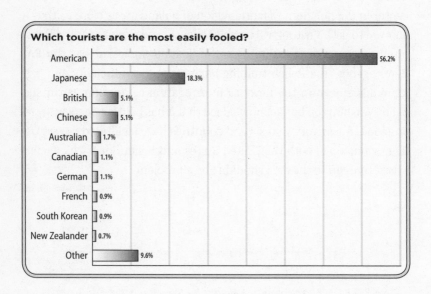

Which tourists are the most easily fooled?

American	56.2%
Japanese	18.3%
British	5.1%
Chinese	5.1%
Australian	1.7%
Canadian	1.1%
German	1.1%
French	0.9%
South Korean	0.9%
New Zealander	0.7%
Other	9.6%

186 THE TITANIC AWARDS

WORST TRAVEL SLOGANS

WINNER

British Columbia's "The Best Place on Earth"

Why not just come right out and tell us how great BC really is?

HONORABLE MENTIONS

- Hilton's "Travel should take you places." (Yes, it should. I think we can all agree on that totally meaningless statement. It would be nicer to say "take you someplace unique," but if you stay in a Hilton, that wouldn't quite work, since the rooms look virtually identical no matter which country you go to.)

- Fargo, North Dakota's "Always warm!" (No, everyone knows it's warm in the summer and you freeze your ass off the rest of the year.)

- "Andalucia: There's only one." If you can't think of anything else to say about a place, this should work.

- "Stockholm: The Capital of Scandinavia." Did they run this by Copenhagen or Oslo? Wars have started over claims like this.

- "Wales: The Big Country." No, Canada is a big country. So is China. And India, Brazil, Australia. If you're going to start making stuff up, why not say Wales is a tropical island with white sandy beaches and attractive, well-tanned natives who serve free beer around the clock?

- Idaho's "Great Potatoes, Tasty Destinations." I think it's time to shake the potato reputation. Yo, Idaho, you may not have noticed, but we can now buy potatoes just about everywhere.

- Minot, North Dakota's "Why Not Minot?" Seriously?! Do you really want us to start thinking of reasons? What happens if people start thinking: "because it's cold as shit and there's not much to do."

- "Malaysia: Truly Asia." As opposed to what—Malaysia, truly Antarctica? But kudos for coming up with the clever rhyme: "aysia" and "asia." Brilliant!

- Israel's "You deserve to be here." Unless you're living in Gaza or the West Bank. C'mon, think of the peace process!

- Washington State's "Say Wa?" Okay, "Wa." Now can I go someplace else? They also had "The place you've been trying to get to," which conjures up an image of a fleet of people driving RVs around the Oregon border trying to find their way in.

- Hamilton, New Zealand's "HamiltON." Hey, clever use of CAPS. Then for your culinary tourism campaign, you can go with "HAMilton," and don't forget "HAmilton" for your comedy festival.

- "Auckland: The Big Little City." Seriously, what does that mean?

- "Panama: It will never leave you." Sounds like you're supposed to go to Panama and get genital herpes.

- Delta Airlines' "Good Goes Around." And around and around and perhaps eventually lands.

- American Airlines' "We know why you fly." Really? You knew about that family gathering I was headed to last year? Or do you mean in general? Like you know we love having to pay for in-flight cuisine? Or do you just want us to think that other airlines have no idea why we take planes?

MOST OVERRATED MAJOR ART MUSEUM

WINNER

The Louvre

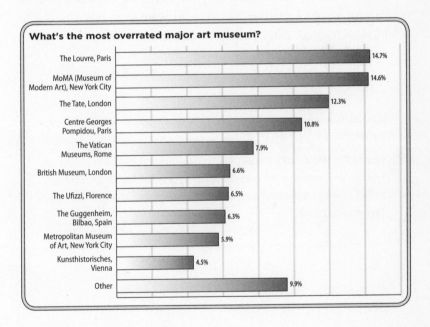

What's the most overrated major art museum?

Museum	Percentage
The Louvre, Paris	14.7%
MoMA (Museum of Modern Art), New York City	14.6%
The Tate, London	12.3%
Centre Georges Pompidou, Paris	10.8%
The Vatican Museums, Rome	7.9%
British Museum, London	6.6%
The Ufizzi, Florence	6.5%
The Guggenheim, Bilbao, Spain	6.3%
Metropolitan Museum of Art, New York City	5.9%
Kunsthistorisches, Vienna	4.5%
Other	9.9%

TITANIC AWARD

WORST TRAVEL REQUEST

WINNER

Some travel requests are a little off the deep end. This one seems to uniquely combine a lame idea with flat-out stupidity. Travel agent Steven Greenbaum of Pisa Brothers Travel in New York was asked to book a trip with a pet Chihuahua. The traveler wanted to take the dog to Chihuahua, Mexico. Why? To help the pet discover his roots.

Source: *Travel + Leisure*, April 2009

PERSONAL WORST

WORST TOURIST INFORMATION OFFICE   *Badaling, China, has a tourist office that only provides information about Beijing (which is a couple hours away). I asked them about a place to stay in Badaling itself, but they said they couldn't help.*

—Brook Silva-Braga, travel documentary filmmaker

MOST OVERRATED CATHEDRAL

WINNER

Notre Dame

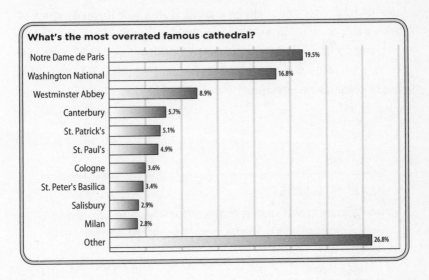

What's the most overrated famous cathedral?

Notre Dame de Paris	19.5%
Washington National	16.8%
Westminster Abbey	8.9%
Canterbury	5.7%
St. Patrick's	5.1%
St. Paul's	4.9%
Cologne	3.6%
St. Peter's Basilica	3.4%
Salisbury	2.9%
Milan	2.8%
Other	26.8%

TITANIC AWARD

WORST TRAVEL ACCESSORY

WINNER

Thomas Pink

Looking for a sign you might be a geek? How about if you own one of these: a silk designer tie with an iPod holder. Thomas Pink, the British shirt brand with 80 shops around the world, introduced the "commuter tie" as part of its main line for autumn and winter 2009–2010. This should come as no surprise: Thomas Pink also has plans for a "commuter shirt."

Source: Reuters, September 18, 2009

PERSONAL WORST

WORST CLICHÉ TRAVEL WRITING LINE ABOUT BEACH/WATER *Any sentence with mentions of powder sand; slices of heaven; and turquoise, indigo, sapphire, ultramarine, glimmering, scintillating water.*

—Eddy Patricelli, editor in chief of *Islands* magazine

RUDEST TOURISTS

WINNER

American

AFRICA/MIDDLE EAST WINNER: Israeli
ASIA WINNER: Chinese
EUROPE WINNER: French
LATIN AMERICA WINNER: Mexican
NORTH AMERICA WINNER: American
PACIFIC WINNER: Australian

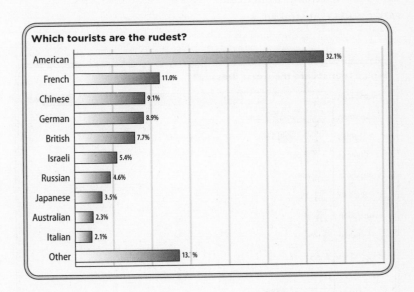

Which tourists are the rudest?

American	32.1%
French	11.0%
Chinese	9.1%
German	8.9%
British	7.7%
Israeli	5.4%
Russian	4.6%
Japanese	3.5%
Australian	2.3%
Italian	2.1%
Other	13. %

TITANIC
SURVEY

WORST-DRESSED TOURISTS

WINNER

American

AFRICA/MIDDLE EAST WINNER: Israeli
ASIA WINNER: Chinese
EUROPE WINNER: German
LATIN AMERICA WINNER: Mexican
NORTH AMERICA WINNER: American
PACIFIC WINNER: Australian

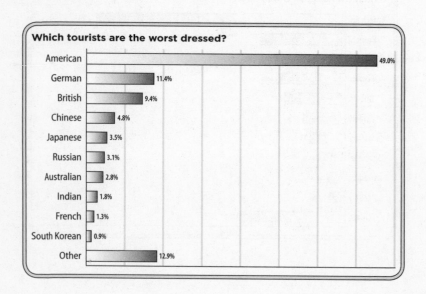

Which tourists are the worst dressed?

Tourist	Percentage
American	49.0%
German	11.4%
British	9.4%
Chinese	4.8%
Japanese	3.5%
Russian	3.1%
Australian	2.8%
Indian	1.8%
French	1.3%
South Korean	0.9%
Other	12.9%

194   THE TITANIC AWARDS

WORST SMELLING MAJOR CITY (OF TOP 100 CITIES)

TITANIC SURVEY

WINNER

Bangkok, Thailand

AFRICA/MIDDLE EAST WINNER: Cairo, Egypt

ASIA WINNER: Bangkok, Thailand

EUROPE WINNER: Paris, France

LATIN AMERICA WINNER: Mexico City, Mexico

NORTH AMERICA WINNER: Los Angeles, California, USA

PACIFIC WINNER: Sydney, Australia

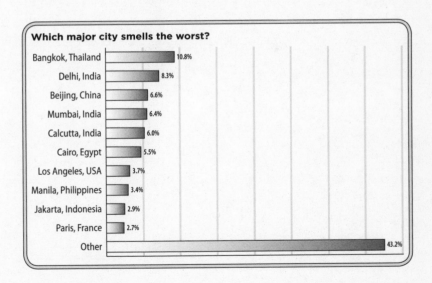

Which major city smells the worst?

City	%
Bangkok, Thailand	10.8%
Delhi, India	8.3%
Beijing, China	6.6%
Mumbai, India	6.4%
Calcutta, India	6.0%
Cairo, Egypt	5.5%
Los Angeles, USA	3.7%
Manila, Philippines	3.4%
Jakarta, Indonesia	2.9%
Paris, France	2.7%
Other	43.2%

TITANIC AWARD

WORST URINAL

WINNER

Old Faithful, Yellowstone National Park

Two workers at Yellowstone National Park were fired after a live web-cam caught them urinating into Old Faithful geyser. The pissing contest cost one man, a 23-year-old, $750, a three-year unsupervised probation, and two years of banishment from Yellowstone. The other employee's case was reported pending. No, the geyser was not erupting at the time.

Source: MSNBC/Associated Press, May 14, 2009

APPENDIX 1

The Major Airlines as Designated by Editor

Aeroflot
AeroMexico
Air Canada
Air China
Air France
Air New Zealand
Alitalia
All Nippon Airways
America West Airlines
American Airlines
ANA
Asiana Airlines
Austrian
bmi
British Airways
Cathay Pacific
China Southern Airlines
Continental Airlines
Delta Air Lines
EgyptAir
Emirates Airline
Iberia
Japan Airlines

KLM Royal Dutch Airlines
Korean Air
LOT Polish Airlines
Lufthansa
Malaysia Airlines
Northwest Airlines
Qantas Airways
SAS
Saudi Airlines
Scandinavian Airlines
Shanghai Airlines
Singapore Airlines
South African Airways
Southwest Airlines
Spanair
Swiss Air
TAP Portugal
Thai Airways
Turkish Airlines
United Airlines
US Airways
Virgin

APPENDIX 2

Top 100 Cities

Picking the 100 largest cities isn't quite as obvious as it seems. There's rarely a city wall that determines where you stop counting. More often, there's "London" and "Greater London," and when you count the surrounding suburbs, the population can more than double. You may find fault with this list, but it does represent a fairly diverse range of the world's larger cities.

Abidjan, Côte d'Ivoire
Addis Ababa, Ethiopia
Ahmedabad, India
Alexandria, Egypt
Alger, Algeria
Almadabad, India
Ankara, Turkey
Athina, Greece
Baghdad, Iraq
Bangalore, India
Bangdung, Indonesia
Bangkok, Thailand
Beijing, China
Belo Horizonte, Brazil
Berlin, Germany
Bogota, Colombia
Buenos Aires, Argentina
Busan, South Korea
Cairo, Egypt
Calcutta, India
Cape Town, South Africa

Caracas, Venezuela
Casablanca, Morocco
Changchun, China
Chengdu, China
Chennai, India
Chicago, Illinois, USA
Chongqing, China
Dalian, China
Dallas, Texas, USA
Delhi, India
Detroit, Michigan, USA
Dhaka, Bangladesh
Düsseldorf, Germany
Essen, Germany
Frankfurt, Germany
Guadalajara, Mexico
Guangzhou, China
Handan, China
Hangzhou, China
Hanoi, Vietnam
Harbin, China

Ho Chi Minh City, Vietnam

Hong Kong, China

Houston, Texas, USA

Hyderabad, India

Istanbul, Turkey

Jakarta, Indonesia

Jeddah, Saudi Arabia

Jinan, China

Johannesburg, South Africa

Karachi, Pakistan

Katowice, Poland

Kinshasa, DRC

Kolkata, India

Köln, Germany

Lahore, Pakistan

Lima, Peru

London, UK

Los Angeles, California, USA

Madrid, Spain

Manila, Philippines

Maputo, Mozambique

Medellin, Colombia

Melbourne, Australia

Mexico City, Mexico

Milano, Italy

Monterrey, Mexico

Montréal, Canada

Moscow, Russian Fed.

Mumbai, India

Nagoya, Japan

Nairobi, Kenya

Nanjing, China

Napoli, Italy

Osaka, Japan

Paris, France

Philadelphia, Pennsylvania, USA

Porto Alegre, Brazil

Pune, India

Pusan, South Korea

Qingdao, China

Recife, Brazil

Rio de Janeiro, Brazil

Riyadh, Saudi Arabia

Saint Petersburg, Russian Fed.

Salvador, Brazil

San Francisco, California, USA

Santiago, Chile

Santo Domingo, Dominican Republic

São Paulo, Brazil

Seoul, South Korea

Shenyang, China

Singapore, Singapore

Surat, India

Sydney, Australia

Tehran, Iran

Tianjin, China

Toronto, Canada

Washington, DC, USA

Wuhan, China

Xi'an, China

Yangon, Myanmar (Burma)

Yokohama, Japan

ACKNOWLEDGMENTS

This book would be a coverless, barely organized, stapled clump of papers if it weren't for my editor, Meg Leder, who patiently helped turn a quirky and unconventional idea into the entertaining collection you now hold in your hands. What's more, she returned calls and emails within seconds, listened, had great ideas, and is by far the best editor I've ever worked with.

Without John Duff, however, the book would have no bar code. John, an avid traveler himself, grasped the concept at once. His input and support for the project have been valuable and much appreciated.

My agent, Michael Bourret, deserves credit for, among other things, coming up with the title of this book. He's one of the most thoughtful, nicest people I've ever worked with, though I'm happy I've never had to bargain with him.

I also want to express my gratitude to the travel writers and editors who were kind enough to share their "worst of" tales and opinions about this project. Thank you.

Finally, I want to thank my three daughters for being so patient with their dad, who was often glued to the computer before deadlines. Thank you for not spilling anything on my keyboard or erasing my files, tempting as it was!

FOR INFORMATION ABOUT
THE TITANIC AWARDS

Calling All Travelers

The Titanic Awards wants your "worst of" experiences, especially photos and videos. There are no hard-and-fast rules for a worst travel experience—whatever strikes you as tacky, wrong, low quality, or evidence of poor judgment. Bad hotel bathrooms, disgusting hotel pools, crazy intersections, bizarre restaurant names, unsafe-looking buses—all good material. Share your rants as well—add them to the comments of similar travel-news items or rants from travel writers and we'll try to highlight them on the main page. Thank you.

TitanicAwards.com